Lepanto 1571

The greatest naval battle of the Renaissance

Campaign • 114

Lepanto 1571

The greatest naval battle of the Renaissance

Angus Konstam · Illustrated by Tony Bryan

Series editor Lee Johnson · *Consultant editor* David G Chandler

First published in Great Britain in 2003 by Osprey Publishing,
Midland House, West Way, Botley, Oxford OX2 0PH, UK
44-02 23rd St, Suite 219, Long Island City, NY 11101, USA
Email: info@ospreypublishing.com

Transferred to digital print on demand 2010

First published 2003
5th impression 2009

Printed and bound by PrintOnDemand-Worldwide.com, Peterborough, UK

A CIP catalogue record for this book is available from the British Library

ISBN: 978 1 84176 409 2

Editorial by Lee Johnson
Design by The Black Spot
Index by Alison Worthington
Maps by The Map Studio
3D bird's-eye views by The Black Spot
Originated by PPS Grasmere Ltd, Leeds, UK
Typeset in Helvetica Neue and ITC New Baskerville

KEY TO MILITARY SYMBOLS

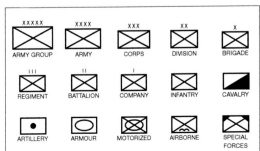

FOR A CATALOGUE OF ALL BOOKS PUBLISHED BY
OSPREY MILITARY AND AVIATION PLEASE CONTACT:

Osprey Direct, c/o Random House Distribution Center,
400 Hahn Road, Westminster, MD 21157
Email: uscustomerservice@ospreypublishing.com

Osprey Direct, The Book Service Ltd, Distribution Centre,
Colchester Road, Frating Green, Colchester,
Essex, CO7 7DW
Email: customerservice@ospreypublishing.com

www.ospreypublishing.com

CONTENTS

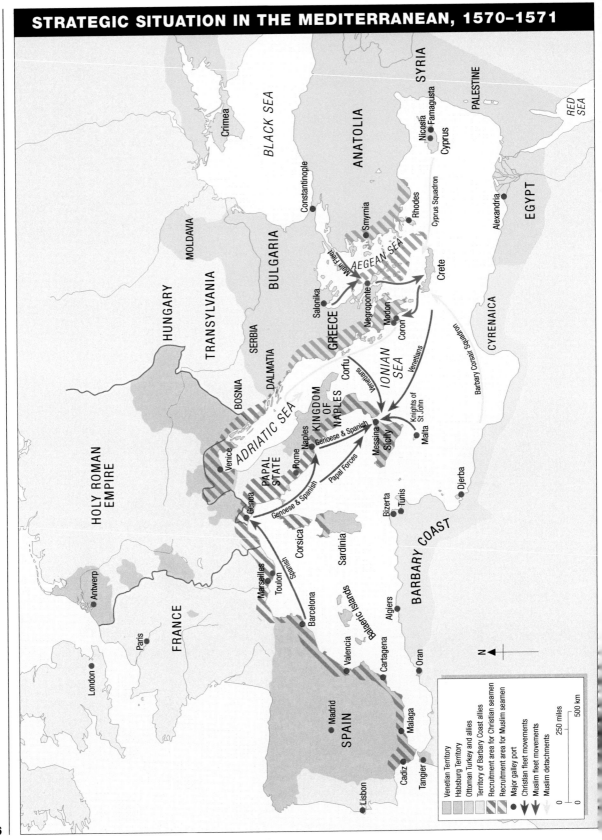

STRATEGIC SITUATION IN THE MEDITERRANEAN, 1570–1571

RED SEA

SYRIA

PALESTINE

BLACK SEA

Crimea

ANATOLIA

Nicosia
Famagusta
Cyprus

Rhodes

EGYPT

Alexandria

Cyprus Squadron

MOLDAVIA

Constantinople

Smyrna

CYRENAICA

HUNGARY

TRANSYLVANIA

BULGARIA

AEGEAN SEA

Crete

SERBIA

GREECE

Salonika

Main Fleet

Negroponte
Modon
Corron

Barbary Corsair Squadron

BOSNIA

DALMATIA

Corfu

IONIAN SEA

Venetians

HOLY ROMAN EMPIRE

ADRIATIC SEA

Venice

PAPAL STATE

KINGDOM OF NAPLES

Naples
Rome

Genoese & Spanish

Messina
Sicily

Knights of St John

Venetians

Malta

Genoa

Papal Forces

Bizerta
Tunis

Djerba

Genoese & Spanish

Corsica

Sardinia

BARBARY COAST

Marseilles
Toulon

Spanish

Barcelona

Balearic Islands

Algiers

FRANCE

Paris

London

Valencia
Cartagena

Oran

Antwerp

N

Madrid

SPAIN

Malaga

Cadiz
Tangier

Lisbon

INTRODUCTION

Cervantes on his galley sets the sword back in the sheath
Don John of Austria rides homeward with a wreath.
And he sees across a weary land a straggling road in Spain,
Up which a lean and foolish knight for ever rides in vain,
And he smiles, but not as Sultans smile, and settles back the blade,
But Don John of Austria rides home from the Crusade.

GK Chesterton **Lepanto**

On a sunny morning in early October 1571, two great fleets slowly approached each other in the blue waters of the Gulf of Patras. Hundreds of vessels, all colourfully decorated with banners, flags and streamers prepared themselves for the coming battle. These were no ordinary warships, and this was no ordinary fight.

The battle of Lepanto that followed can be seen as the last great Crusade, a culmination of eight centuries of warfare between the forces of Christianity and Islam. The battle was the climax of a struggle for supremacy in the Mediterranean, but Lepanto also marked the end of an era. For centuries, war galleys were the primary fighting vessel in the Mediterranean Sea; craft that bore a passing resemblance to the oared warships used by the Ancient Greeks and Romans. Few of the sailors, soldiers, gunners, oarsmen and galley slaves who waited for the battle to begin were aware that this would be the last great galley battle. Improvements in naval artillery had already pushed the development of the galley to its limits. The sailing warship of the Atlantic was making inroads into the Mediterranean, and within a decade or so, the galley would become obsolete, replaced by well-armed sailing men-of-war.

Since the end of the Byzantine Empire with the fall of Constantinople in 1453, the territorial expansion of the Ottoman Turks had been dramatic, pushing up the Danube valley and down through Greece. The inexorable advance of Turkish troops had gone virtually unchecked, bringing the army of the Turkish sultan to the gates of Vienna, and the power of this new Muslim superpower to its zenith. The Lepanto campaign itself had begun as a result of a Turkish invasion of Venetian-held Cyprus the year before, and for the Christians the battle was an attempt to stop this maritime expansion before the Turkish galleys threatened Venice, Naples and Rome. Spain was a rival superpower, but her interests were diverse, and much of her overseas territory lay outside the Mediterranean, in the Americas or in north-western Europe. Consequently the war against Islam played a minor part in Spanish affairs after the fall of Granada in 1492. The same year saw Christopher Columbus sail in search of the Indies, only to discover America. For the next seven decades, the Spanish conquered, colonised and exploited the lands, people and resources of central and

southern America, and used the profits from this imperial adventure to fund political and military initiatives in Europe. A superpower dependent on the flow of silver from Mexico and Peru, the Spanish Empire was built on a shaky foundation. Increasingly, her economic lifeline came under attack from interlopers such as the English, French and Dutch. Consequently, much of Spain's military and naval resources were committed to the protection of the Spanish overseas empire, and warfare with her northern European enemies.

To the Spanish, the Mediterranean may have been something of an economic and military backwater, but the region played a vital part in Spanish policy. Since 1495 France and Spain had been locked in an intermittent war for control of Italy. The decisive Spanish (and Imperial) victory at Pavia in 1525 and the Imperialist sack of Rome four years later ushered in a new era in Italian politics, where the peninsula would be dominated by Spanish and Imperialist policies. Although the Habsburg–Valois war between Spain and France would continue until 1559, the French were excluded from Italy, and from interference in Italian politics.

With the other European superpower distracted in its war with France, the Ottoman Turks were free to continue their advance, and while the Spanish were ensuring their political domination of Italy, the Turks were busy incorporating the Barbary States of North Africa into the Ottoman sphere. This string of piratical settlements was given a boost in 1492, when the Moors expelled from Spain settled in Africa and continued their war against the Spanish by maritime rather than military means. The capture of Algiers in 1516 gave the Barbary Pirates (Corsairs) a secure base, and despite their political and military alliance with the Turks, the Barbary Corsairs continued to wage their own private war against the Christian

The importance of the battle of Lepanto was that it marked the end of a century of Turkish expansion in the Mediterranean, and foreshadowed the political eclipse of the Ottoman Empire as a regional superpower. This depiction of the battle was produced as a celebration of the Christian victory, but stands testimony to the ferocity of the struggle. (Civici Musei, Veneziani d'arte e di storia, Venice)

states of the western Mediterranean. In effect, following the defeat of Christian galley fleets at Prevesa (1538) and Djerba (1560), the Ottoman Turks maintained control of the eastern and central Mediterranean, while their Barbary allies vied for control of the western regions of the sea.

It was becoming increasingly clear to both the Spanish and the other Christian states with a Mediterranean coastline that the Turks needed to be stopped. The Turkish siege of Malta (1565) was the first serious check suffered by the Ottomans in the Mediterranean, and bought the Christian states a breathing space. However, internal divisions between Venetians, Maltese, the Knights of Malta, the Spanish and other smaller Spanish satellite states meant that any real unity was unlikely. As long as the threat remained intangible, united action remained an impossible dream. What tipped the scales was the renewal of the Ottoman Turkish campaign of expansion in 1570.

The Turkish attack on Venetian-held Cyprus prompted the Doge of Venice to appeal to the Pope for help. Only the Pontiff was capable of uniting the various political states into a single body, and overriding the animosity between Venice and the western Mediterranean Christian states. Through extensive diplomatic negotiation, and the calling of what was virtually a crusade against Islam, Pope Pius V created the Holy League, a force capable of standing up to the Turks. That is, it could if the Pope and his lieutenants managed to hold the fragile alliance together. The campaign of 1570 was a disaster for the Holy League, and as they prepared to fight a decisive battle at Lepanto the following year, few felt confident of the outcome. The irresistible force of Islam was about to meet the all too movable object of the Christian alliance. The outcome could well decide the fate of Italy and, ultimately, control of the entire Mediterranean.

Virtually everyone present that morning knew the importance of the coming battle, and it must have been with considerable apprehension that the men in the fleets looked towards their opponents, and the slowly shrinking strip of water between them.

CHRONOLOGY

1565

September Turkish defeat at the Siege of Malta.

1566

January War declared between Ottoman Empire and Holy Roman Empire.
8 September Death of Sultan Süleyman I 'the Magnificent'.
October Accession of Selim II 'the Sot'.

1568

February Peace signed between Ottoman Empire and Holy Roman Empire.

1569

March Start of *Morisco* revolt in southern Spain.
July The Arsenal in Venice damaged by fire.
August Tunis captured by Turks.

1570

February War declared between Ottoman Empire and Venetian Republic.
1 July Turkish troops land on Cyprus.
22 July Nicosia besieged by Mustapha Pasha's army.
15 July Venetians petition Pope Pius V for support.
1 September Christian Fleet rendezvous in Crete.
9 September Nicosia falls and inhabitants massacred.
14 September Christian fleet sails towards Cyprus via Asia Minor.
18 September The Turkish army besieges Famagusta.
19 September News reaches Christian fleet of fall of Nicosia. Decision made to abandon the planned attack against the Turkish fleet off Cyprus.

1571

26 January Antonio Quirini breaks through blockade to reinforce Famagusta.
1 May Start of Mustapha Pasha's bombardment of Famagusta.
25 May Formation of the Holy League.
4 July Turkish fleet under Ali Pasha arrives off Corfu. Turkish raids along Adriatic coast continue all month.
4 August Surrender of Famagusta. Murder of garrison and its commander.
8 August Turkish fleet establishes new base at Lepanto.

16 September Holy League Fleet departs from Messina.
27 September The Holy League Fleet arrives off Corfu.
30 September Dissent in Christian fleet while at anchor off Gomenizza.
3 October Holy League Fleet sails south towards Gulf of Corinth.
4 October Turkish Council of War. Decision made to give battle.
6 October Turks in Gulf of Patras, Christians off Ithaca.

7 October, 1571 BATTLE OF LEPANTO.
07.30 The Christian Fleet passes Scropha Point. The two fleets sight each other.
08.00 Both fleets adopt their battle formation.
10.00 The two fleets begin their advance. A light westerly wind springs up.
10.20 The *galleasses* open fire.
10.30 The first damage is inflicted to a Turkish galley.
10.40 The northern wings clash south of Scropha Point.
11.00 Uluch Ali alters course of the Turkish left wing slightly to the south-west.
11.10 Andrea Doria reacts by altering the course of his Christian right wing to the south-east.
11.15 The Christian left wing outflanks then envelops the Turkish right wing, pinning it against the shoals off Scropha Point.
11.40 The central wings clash, and fighting centres around the two flagships.
11.45 Approximate time of Barbarigo's death in the northern engagement.
Noon Uluch Ali changes course of part of his formation to shoot between the Christian centre and right wing. The fighting in the central and northern sectors reaches a peak.
12.10 A portion of the Christian southern wing heads north-east to intercept Uluch Ali.
12.20 The Turks board Don John's flagship, but are repulsed. The fighting in the centre now focuses on the two fleet flagships.
Uluch Ali's squadron clashes with galleys sent to block his path, and he inflicts significant losses on his opponents. Despite this tactical success, he is unable to influence events in the centre.
Christians attack the flagships of Ali Pasha and Pertau Pasha, anchoring the Turkish centre.
12.30 Pertau Pasha's *lanterna* is captured by the Christians, marking the turning point in the battle for the centre. By this stage the Turks are clearly losing the fight, and are forced onto the defensive.
13.00 *Capitana* of Malta captured by Uluch Ali, forcing both Bazán and Andrea Doria to commit forces to recover it. The Turkish fleet flagship is captured. Death of Ali Pasha.

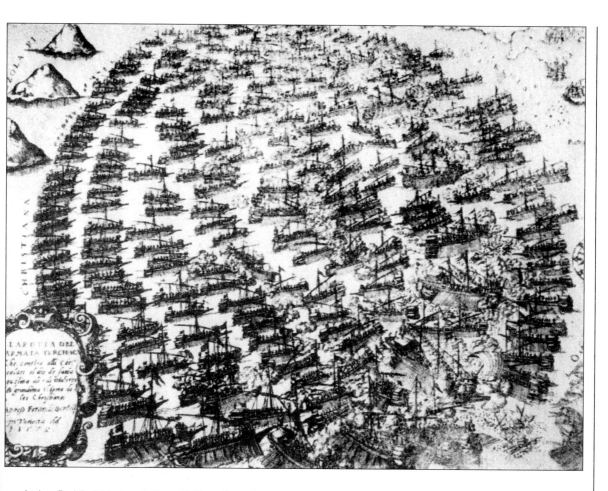

Andrea Doria's right wing clashes with the galleys of Uluch Ali.

13.10 Uluch Ali breaks off the fight, abandoning his embattled galleys to escape with the remains of his squadron. Collapse of the Turkish centre.

14.00 Uluch Ali's squadron escapes to the west. Elsewhere, the Christians capture or sink the remaining Turkish galleys in the centre.

15.00 The fighting ends. Venetian land troops to capture Turks stranded on Scropha Point.

19.00 The Christian Fleet reaches its overnight anchorage at Porta Petala.
Te Deum sung to celebrate Christian victory.

December Meeting of Holy League representatives in Rome. Discussion concerning future operations.

1572

February Plans laid for Levant Campaign by Don John.

April Start of the 'Dutch Revolt'. Spain distracted by events in the Netherlands.

May Death of Pope Pius V. Pope Gregory XIII less enthusiastic about Turkish 'crusade'.

June Venetians murder their leading Turkish prisoners.

July Uluch Ali puts to sea at head of Turkish fleet of 200 new galleys.

August St Bartholomew's Day Massacre in Paris. French distracted by commencement of new phase of the Wars of Religion.

September Indecisive naval campaign off Peloponnese (Morea). Turks able to avoid further losses.

1573

April Peace Treaty between Republic of Venice and Ottoman Turkey.

June Don John captures Tunis from Barbary Corsairs.

1574

September Uluch Ali recaptures Tunis on behalf of Barbary Corsairs.

1577

November Ceasefire agreed between Ottoman Turks and Spanish.

OPPOSING COMMANDERS

RULERS

Before examining the individual commanders who participated in the battle, it is worth mentioning the role played by the rulers of both the Ottoman Turkish Empire and the Holy Roman Empire. **Süleyman (Suleiman) I 'the Magnificent'** who reigned from 1520 to 1566 was the true architect of the Lepanto campaign, having been responsible for the westward expansion of the Ottoman Empire on land. Although by the end of his reign he was not directly involved in military expeditions, the Sultan encouraged any campaign that would expand his borders or influence. When he died in 1566 he was succeeded by Selim II 'the Sot', the son of his favourite wife. Selim continued his father's policy by initiating the operations that would lead directly to the invasion of Cyprus, and the subsequent campaign of Lepanto. Historians have argued that if he had left the campaign to his fleet commanders, the disaster at Lepanto might have been averted, but he considered himself a grand strategist in his father's image, and insisted on dictating both strategy and operational policy. This is surprising, as in most other areas he preferred to leave the day-to-day affairs of state to his father's old Grand Vizier, Sokullu Mehmed Pasha, who held office from 1565 until 1579.

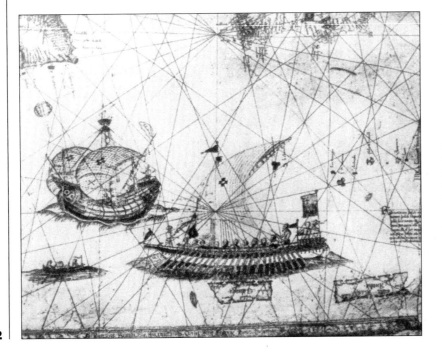

In 1571 the galley as a form of warship was about to be superseded by the sailing warship, capable of mounting a far superior suite of ordnance. In this detail of a Portuguese map of the mid-16th century, a Portuguese galley is shown alongside a small 'carvel' that would soon develop into the larger 'roundship', which were virtually immune to attack by oared galleys by virtue of its all-round defence. (Stratford Archive)

King Philip II of Spain (who reigned from 1556 to 1600) was the most powerful monarch in Christian Europe, despite the division of his father's empire into a Spanish and an Austrian portion. He was encouraged to join forces with the Venetians and the Papacy to form the Holy League by Pope Pius V, who reigned from 1566 to 1572, the staunchest advocate of a naval 'crusade' against the Ottoman Turks. Philip's gift was his ability to appoint the right people. His decision to make his half-brother Don John of Austria the commander of the Fleet of the Holy League was an inspired choice, as he had the diplomatic skills necessary to hold the Christian alliance together. Another key element in the Christian command was the backing of both the Pope and the Doge of Venice for the campaign, as both men realised the need for a joint Christian opposition to Turkish expansionism. Neither the Papacy nor the Venetian Republic could face the Turks alone, and both leaders were willing to do whatever it took to keep Philip II and his allies in the alliance. While all three rulers meddled in the affairs of their national contingents, they all relied on Don John to ensure that the Fleet of the Holy League remained a cohesive naval force, and were reluctant to do anything which would upset the fragile Christian alliance.

CHRISTIAN

Don John (Juan) of Austria (1547–78). The illegitimate son of the Emperor Charles V (who ruled from 1516 to 1556), Don John was the half-brother of King Philip II of Spain (who reigned 1556–1600). His royal blood ensured his position as a leading figure within the Holy Roman Empire. Despite his youth and the handicap of his illegitimate birth, he proved to be a skilled diplomat, and an able military commander. He served as a cavalry commander in both Spain and the Spanish Netherlands, but Philip II had even greater plans for him. He was given an independent military command in 1570 when he suppressed the *Morisco*[1] revolt in Spain. This success, combined with his proven record as a diplomat, led to his appointment as the Captain General of the Fleet of the Holy League in 1571. During the battle of Lepanto he proved to be an inspirational leader, although by leading his flagship, the *Real*, into the thick of the fighting, he effectively handed responsibility for the course of the battle to the Spanish contingent commander, Don Álvaro de Bazán. After his victory at Lepanto, Don John campaigned in North Africa and in Italy before becoming the Imperial Governor of the Spanish Netherlands in 1576. Like General Eisenhower's role in the Second World War, the post of commander of the Fleet of the Holy League required diplomatic skills more than military ones, and it is to his credit that he succeeded in holding the fragile Christian alliance together during the Lepanto campaign.

Agostin Barbarigo (c.1500–1571). The second-in-command of the Venetian contingent of the Fleet of the Holy League, Barbarigo was a competent commander, and a more patient and diplomatic figure than his superior, Sebastian Venier. When Venier threatened to withdraw the Venetian fleet from the alliance, Barbarigo worked with Don John of

Süleyman I 'the Magnificent' (1520–66) was the architect of the aggressive Turkish policy of expansion in the Mediterranean. He was determined that the Turkish repulse at Malta in 1565 was not to be the high water mark of Turkish expansionism, and his son attempted to continue his father's policy. (Topkapi Sarayi Muzei, Istanbul)

---

1 Spain's Islamic population had been forced to convert to Christianity or leave the country. These 'converted' Muslims were called *Moriscos* by the Christian Spanish. In many cases the conversion was superficial and previous customs and dress were retained.

Although the battle of Lepanto involved a certain amount of operational manoeuvring, it soon developed into a close-fought melee between the two fleets, as the opponents tried to ram, board or fire on the enemy in a confused clash of galleys. This depiction is inaccurate in that the fighting was far more compact, and combatants could literally walk from ship to ship. Detail from 'The Battle of Lepanto', a painting by the Italian School, late 16th century. (National Maritime Museum, Greenwich, London)

Austria to hold the alliance together. He then replaced Venier as the Venetian representative in Fleet Councils of War during the latter stages of the Lepanto campaign. Although softly spoken and unprepossessing, he was a highly experienced naval commander, having served in the Venetian galley fleet since his youth. He commanded the left wing of the Christian fleet during the Battle of Lepanto, and intuitively knew how to get the most out of the tactical situation he found himself in. He was killed in the battle.

Marc Antonio Colonna (1535–84), Duke of Tagliacozzo and Paliano. An experienced Italian *Condottiere*, Colonna served in the Spanish army in Italy for much of his life, becoming the Grand Constable of Naples as a result of his loyalty to his Spanish paymasters. A soldier and diplomat rather than a naval commander, Colonna was not the obvious choice for the appointment as Captain General of the Papal Fleet in 1570–71. Despite his lack of naval experience, Colonna was both an Italian and a Spanish soldier, and was therefore well placed to help encourage Philip II to join the Holy League. His appointment by Pope Pius V(1566–72) was therefore instrumental in the creation of the Fleet of the Holy League, and he continued to help Don John of Austria bind the alliance together throughout the campaign. During the battle he fought in the central division, and supported Don John with as much military skill as he had with his diplomatic talents in the preceding months.

Sebastian Venier (also written as 'Veniero')(c.1497–1572). The Captain General of Venice during the Lepanto campaign, the Venetian nobleman gained his command following the failure of his predecessor during the 1570 campaign. Although he was a capable commander, his animosity towards the Genoese in general and Gian Andrea Doria in particular almost tore the Holy League apart. A proud Venetian, he was a staunch defender of Venetian rights within the alliance, and resented any attempt to place Spanish troops on his undermanned galleys to bolster their strength. At one stage, when he was told that Andrea Doria would inspect the Venetian contingent, he threatened to kill the Genoese *Condottiere*, and any of his men who set foot on board his flagship. His stance threatened to cause irrevocable rifts within the alliance, and Alvise Mocenigo I, the Doge of Venice (who reigned 1570–77), was forced to intervene, ordering Agostin Barbarigo to represent Venice in all Fleet Councils of War. During the battle, Venier fought in the centre, and proved a brave and capable galley commander.

Gian Andrea Doria (1539–1606), Prince of Melfi. The great-nephew of the famous Genoese Naval *Condottiere* Andrea Doria (1466–1560), he became the heir to the Dorian naval legacy in 1560, when he was named Philip II's Captain General at Sea in the Mediterranean following the death of his famous namesake. In 1560, his first year of command, he was defeated by the Ottoman Admiral (Kapudan Pasha) Piali Pasha (1520–71) at Djerba, off the coast of Tunisia. His reputation was restored during the following decade, but he was still mistrusted by the Venetians. As a naval *Condottiere*, he raised his own galley fleet for service with his Imperial patron despite a growing reliance on state-owned fleets. At Lepanto he commanded the right wing (or vanguard) of the Christian fleet. A skilled seaman, he preferred to fight a battle of manoeuvre rather than rely on brute force. Although criticised for the time he took to begin the fight (charges of cowardice or duplicity were levelled against him), he performed his duties competently, despite being outwitted by Uluch Ali, his Turkish opponent. The controversy surrounding his actions has tarnished his reputation ever since.

Don Álvaro de Bazán (1526–88). The son of Charles V's Captain General of Galleys, Don Álvaro came from a distinguished line of Spanish naval commanders, and inherited his father's command in 1559. He distinguished himself as a galley commander in the decade preceding the battle of Lepanto, and was given the title of Marquéz of Santa Cruz in 1569 as a reward for his services. He served as the titular commander of the Spanish galley contingent during the Lepanto campaign, and was given command of the Reserve Division for the battle. His reputation as the leading Spanish admiral of his day was well deserved, and he fed galleys and men into the front line with great skill during the fighting, yet still retained enough of a reserve to react to Uluch Ali's breakout attempt towards the close of the engagement. After Lepanto he was given command of Philip II's Atlantic fleet during his invasion of Portugal (1580), and went on to defeat the French in the battle of Punta Delgada (1582) during the struggle for the Azores. Although given command of the Spanish Armada, he died in 1588, before the fleet sailed to attack England.

TURKISH

Müezzenade Ali Pasha (1522–71). Ali Pasha, named 'Müezzenade' (Son of the Caller to Prayers) was born in Anatolia, and gained promotion as a diplomat and administrator in Ottoman Turkish service. Reputedly of

Selim II 'the Sot' (reigned 1566–75) succeeded to the Turkish throne through the intrigues of his mother, Süleyman's favourite wife Hurrem, and although he was in favour of continuing his father's aggressive policy of expansion, he left the running of most military and naval matters to his advisers. (Topkapi Sarayi Muzei, Istanbul).

Uluch Ali Pasha (c.1511–1587) was an Italian, but converted to Islam after being captured by the Barbary Corsairs. He rose to command his own galley, and by 1568 he had become the Bey of Algiers, the ruler of the Barbary Coast. He commanded the Turkish left wing at Lepanto, and was the only senior Turkish commander to survive the battle. (Museo Storica Navale, Venice)

'Müezzenade' Ali Pasha (1522–71) was given command of the Turkish fleet following the dismissal of his predecessor in January 1571. He was reluctant to join battle with the Christians, but was swayed by the opinions of his subordinates, the inaccurate reports of his scouts and the aggressive orders from the Turkish court. This (probably inaccurate) depiction of the Turkish commander was produced in Germany in order to satisfy public curiosity. (Author's Collection)

RIGHT The Coronation of Pope Pius V in 1566 was a pivotal event in the history of the war between Christians and Muslims in the Mediterranean, as in Pius the Sultan found an implacable enemy. One of the principal exponents of a new crusade, the Pope was the mastermind behind the formation of the Holy League. He served as Pontiff until his death in 1572. Bas relief from the Basilica Santa Maria Maggiore, Rome. (Stratford Archive)

low birth, according to tradition he followed his father's vocation, calling the faithful to prayer in Constantinople until his voice attracted the wife of the Sultan. Under her patronage he was introduced into the Turkish court, and prospered through his own skills as a courtier. Like his Christian counterpart at Lepanto, he was a diplomat as much as a naval commander, having served as the Governor of Egypt (1563–66). His military and naval experience was also extensive, having participated in the Djerba campaign of 1560, and then in the siege of Malta (1565), where he commanded Egyptian contingents. He went on to serve as the deputy to the Turkish fleet commander (Kapudan Pasha) in the Mediterranean, Piali Pasha, during the Cyprus campaign of 1570–71, and following the dismissal of Piali Pasha in January 1571, Ali Pasha became the new commander of the Turkish fleet. He served in this capacity during the Lepanto campaign, and was killed in the closing stages of the battle. He was renowned as a bowman, and when battle was joined he fought the Christians from his flagship amongst the ranks of his fellow Muslim archers. Although an able commander, he was constrained by the aggressive orders of his Sultan to fight the Christians regardless of the risk to his fleet. In other circumstances, he might have been able to choose a better place and time to fight, and therefore alter the outcome of the campaign.

Mehmet Sulik Pasha (c.1525–71). A General more than a naval commander, Sulik Pasha (known as 'Sirocco') was an Egyptian, and commanded the galley squadron of Alexandria and Egypt (some 20 galleys, and eight *fustas*). He entered military service at 17, fighting on both land and sea for the next two decades, and was rewarded with the position of Bey of Alexandria in 1562. He participated in the siege of Malta (1565), and was reputedly a skilled governor of Egypt and a gifted diplomat, with devout religious beliefs. He led a contingent of Egyptian galleys in the Cyprus campaign of 1570 and took part in siege operations at Famagusta. At Lepanto he commanded the right wing of the Muslim fleet, but he failed to out-manoeuvre his Venetian counterpart, and his outflanking move led to the loss of his division. Although he escaped the debacle, he was severely wounded in the fighting, and was captured on Malcantone by his enemies. Mortally wounded, he asked to be spared further agony, and was duly killed by his Venetian captors on the day after the battle.

Uluch Ali Pasha (c.1511–87). Originally born as Giovan Dionigi in Italian Calabria, the man who would become Uluch (also 'Uluj') Ali was captured by the Barbary Corsair Giafer while fishing off the Italian coast, and became a galley slave. He adopted the Muslim faith, and as a free man he rapidly gained advancement. He rose to command his own Algerian *galiot* during the 1550s, and was given command of a squadron-sized force during the Djerba campaign. He played a leading part in the Christian defeat at Djerba (1560), and went on to command the Barbary Coast contingent of the Turkish fleet during the Malta campaign of 1565–66. By 1566 he had replaced Turgut Rais as Governor of Tripoli, and two years later he was appointed as Bey of Algiers, campaigning against the Spanish at Tunis. He inflicted a minor defeat on the Knights of Malta in 1570 before joining forces with the main Turkish fleet for the Lepanto campaign. During the battle he commanded the left wing of the Muslim fleet, and fought with distinction, managing to extricate himself from the battle along with a small force of galleys. The Sultan appointed Uluch Ali as the Commander of the Turkish Navy for the 1572 campaign, and he managed to rebuild the Muslim galley fleet, then held the Christians at bay until the Holy League dissolved in 1573. He went on to recapture Tunis (1574), and served as supreme Turkish naval commander in the Mediterranean until his death.

Amurat Dragut Rais (c.1535–71). Little is known about the commander of the Reserve Division of the Muslim fleet. It is considered likely that he was the son of the veteran Turkish naval commander Turgut Rais (1506–65), and served as a naval squadron commander during the Malta campaign (1565–66) and in the Cyprus campaign (1570). He was killed in the battle.

Don John of Austria (1547–78) was only 24 when he led the Christian fleet into battle at Lepanto as the Captain General of the Fleet of the Holy League, but he compensated for his lack of military experience with excellent diplomatic skills. The fragile Christian alliance was held together largely through his efforts and leadership. (Civici Musei Veneziani d'arte e di storia, Venice)

OPPOSING FLEETS

THE GALLEY

E
ven before the two fleets clashed at Lepanto, the galley had become obsolete – a warship type that had developed beyond the ability of the Mediterranean infrastructure to perpetually support it. As Guilmartin (1974) put it, the Renaissance war galley was akin to a dinosaur. Its development reached a peak in the mid-16th century, and although larger and better-armed galleys were developed, these required a greater proportion of resources than ordinary galleys. As reliable bronze guns became more readily available, larger and more powerful gun batteries were mounted on galleys. This altered the delicate balance between speed and manpower (or oarsmen). A larger hull was required, and more rowers. This in turn created greater limitations on the operational range of the vessel, as the supplies of food and water needed to sustain it increased in proportion. Similarly, the cost of these vessels increased exponentially. On top of this the cost of wages increased throughout both the Muslim and Christian regions of the Mediterranean during the later 16th century, leading to an increased reliance on the use of galley slaves as oarsmen. For the most part the Venetians still used free citizen oarsmen, but the majority of oarsmen in all other Mediterranean galley fleets were prisoners; either enemy captives or criminals[2]. This meant an increased need for reliable soldiers, as galley slaves needed to be guarded, and took no part in any fighting. At the same time, the ready availability of artillery that led to a general increase in galley size also permitted the creation of armed sailing ships. Unlike galleys, these sailing 'carracks' or 'roundships' could carry a broadside armament, and were capable of virtually all-round defence. This made them practically invulnerable to galleys, unless they were becalmed and could be outmanoeuvred. This alone would have led to the extinction of the war galley. When the advent of the sailing warship was coupled with the increasingly prohibitive costs involved in maintaining a galley fleet, the writing was on the wall. The warships at Lepanto represented both the pinnacle of galley development and the end of an era.

The fleets themselves comprised several types of galley. The *gallia sotil* (ordinary galley) was the most common galley type to participate in the battle – excluding the Turkish *fustas*, 80 per cent of the combined fleets were ordinary galleys. A typical Venetian *galia sottil* was 41m (137ft) long, and just over 5m (17ft) wide, with a draft of 1.2m (4ft) and a displacement of 200 tons. She carried a large centreline gun in her bow battery, flanked by two lighter pieces. For the most part the Venetians still used the *alla sensile* rowing system where a single oarsman pulled each oar, which were

Alvise Moncenigo I, the Doge of Venice (reigned 1570–77), realised that the Venetians alone were incapable of resisting the Turkish conquest of Cyprus, or even stopping them from dominating the Adriatic Sea. Consequently he was instrumental in the creation of the Holy League, and in its survival as a political and military entity. (Archivo Fotografico Caceres)

---

2 The use of galley slaves was a new phenomenon in Turkish fleets and Turkish concerns about controlling Christian slaves in battle (see p.30) demonstrate their inexperience in the use of large numbers of galley slaves. For details on the crewing of Mediterranean war galleys see New Vanguard 62 *Renaissance War Galley 1470–1590*.

grouped in three banks. A typical Venetian galley had 24 oars in each bank for a total of 72 oars per side, requiring a total of 144 oarsmen. Other galleys were different, as most had gone over to the *alla scaloccio* (ladder style) method, which was far less efficient that the traditional method, but allowed the use of galley slaves rather than wage-earning oarsmen. In this system, four men operated each oar (one free man, and three slaves), and the typical galley carried 24 oars per side (192 oarsmen). This method had become standard by 1571, and was becoming increasingly common in the Venetian fleet. Although the *galia sottil* of all nationalities were similar, subtle national differences could be determined. Put simply, the Spanish placed a greater emphasis on a powerful artillery battery and the use of the galley as a vehicle for carrying troops, while both the Venetians and Turks favoured the retention of mobility and speed, at the cost of fighting potential. This meant that while most Venetian and Turkish galleys carried a bow armament of one large centreline gun, two flanking guns and a battery of swivel pieces, Spanish, Neapolitan and some Genoese galleys carried four flanking guns, giving them a greater weight of shot fired from their bow battery.

Squadron and fleet commanders often used galleys that were larger than usual, or were provided with a large bow battery. These were the *lanternas*, named after the large lanterns mounted on their sterns, used for signalling and recognition. These were often the largest vessels in a fleet; symbols of authority with numerous banks of oars and large contingents of soldiers. For example, the *Real* (Royal) of Don John had 35 banks of oars, but with a *ciurma* (rowing crew) of 210 oarsmen, with six men to each oar, rowing in the *alla scaloccio* manner. Large galleys also served as the *Pretronas* (squadron leader; *Capitana* in Spanish), and acted as flagships of smaller national contingents in the fleet, such as the Papacy, the Knights of St John, or *assentiste* (condottieri commanders) such as Andrea Doria. *Bastardas* were larger-than-average versions of the *galia sottil*, but these were rarely listed separately from other ordinary galleys.

The *galiot* was a smaller version of the *galia sottil*, with 16–20 oars per side. These craft were rowed *a scaloccio*, with two men to each oar, and had a low freeboard, which made them vulnerable when fighting full-sized galleys. Their big advantage was speed, meaning they could usually avoid contact with larger vessels. A typical *galiot* was 27m (87ft) long with a beam of 3m (10ft) and a draft of less than 2m (6.5ft). A 20-bank Turkish *galiot* carried 60–80 oarsmen, supported by 40–60 soldiers, and a handful of gunners. It usually only carried a single centreline gun (a 16–24-pdr piece) supported by a small bank of swivel guns. The Turks also employed 64 *fustas*. These were tiny oared craft with 10–15 banks of oars per side. Like the *galiot*, the *fusta* was rowed *a scaloccio* with two oarsmen per bank, and carried up to 60 oarsmen and 30–40 soldiers. A typical *fusta* was 21.5m (70ft)long, and was armed with a single centreline gun (a 12–18-pdr). The *fusta* was considered too small to participate in a battle, but was useful when moving reinforcements and reserves around behind the main galley line while it was in action.

The six *galleasses* in the Christian fleet virtually amounted to a secret weapon, and represented the ultimate development of the oared warship. A Venetian invention, the *galleass* was seen as a counter to the sailing warship and to large Spanish galleys. Although powerful, its lack of manoeuvrability meant that it was of limited use in battle. Converted

Gian Andrea Doria (1539–1606) was one of the most experienced naval commanders in the Christian fleet, and the most controversial. He was accused of cowardice following his performance at Lepanto, as he appeared unwilling to close with the Turkish left wing. It is more likely that he was simply trying to outmanoeuvre his wily Turkish opponent, Uluch Ali. (Museo Naval, Genoa-Pegli)

Agostino Barbarigo (c.1500–71) was an experienced Venetian commander who led the Christian left wing during the battle. Although his galleys were victorious, he was mortally wounded during the closing stages of the fight. Original in the Cleveland Museum of Art. (Clyde Hensley Collection)

Sebastian Venier (c.1497–1572) was the Captain General of the Venetian contingent during the Lepanto campaign. Although he was a highly experienced naval commander, he aggressively resisted any attempts by non-Venetian members of the alliance to interfere in the running, organisation and discipline of his Venetian fleet. Painting by Tintoretto. (Archivo Fotografico Caceres)

Another depiction of Sebastian Venier (also written 'Veniero'). His distrust of the Genoese created major diplomatic problems for Don John and Marc Antonio Colonna, particularly when his execution of Spanish officers off Corfu almost led to war between the Venetian and Spanish-Genoese contingents of the Christian fleet. (Kuntshistorisches Museum, Vienna)

using the hulls of old *galia grosse* (merchant galleys), the seven Venetian *galleasses* developed in time for the Lepanto campaign averaged 47m (152ft) long, with an 8m (26ft) beam. They were powered in the *alla scaloccio* fashion, with 25 banks per side, and 5 oarsmen per oar. In addition they carried 250–300 soldiers, plus 70 sailors to work the sails. A rounded forecastle was fitted in place of the usual galley gun platform, and up to nine heavy guns were fitted in this wooden fortress. Additional artillery was placed on broadside mounts and in the stern. While fitted with masts and sails, these were primarily oared fighting craft, but their slow, lumbering and ungainly qualities meant that at Lepanto, the six *galleasses* present were hard-pressed to take up their appointed positions before the battle commenced.

THE RIVAL FLEETS

Both fleets at Lepanto had a virtually identical number of galleys. The fleet of the Holy League boasted 206 galleys, plus six *galleasses*. As already noted, galley sizes and crew allocations varied, but a typical *galia sottil* required a *ciurma* of about 200 oarsmen to operate the vessel. The larger *lanternas* required a proportionately larger crew, while the *galleasses* needed a minimum of 320 oarsmen and sailors. As for soldiers, the typical *galia sottil* carried 125 soldiers on board, but at Lepanto these numbers varied widely. The Venetians were under strength in both soldiers and oarsmen, prompting Don John to order Sebastian Venier to take on board Italian and Spanish soldiers to augment his crews. A document mentions the Venetians having a mere 75 soldiers per galley when they arrived off Corfu, but once Venier was forced to take on foreign troops, and once men were stripped from the Corfu garrison, the situation improved. Fifteen hundred Spaniards and 2,500 Italians were distributed throughout the Venetian fleet, meaning that on average each Venetian galley carried approximately 80 soldiers (50 Venetian and 30 others). The average Spanish strength was 145 soldiers per galley, while the Papal and Genoese vessels carried 120–130 soldiers each. Obviously, *lanternas* carried larger contingents of troops.

The following soldiers were reported as being available for service in the fleet before the battle: 5,000 Venetian, 1,500 Papal, 5,000 German, 8,000 Spanish, 5,000 Italian and 4,000 gentlemen adventurers for a total of 28,500 soldiers. Given that the fleet contained about 40,000 sailors and oarsmen, the total Christian force amounted to just under 70,000 men.

The Turks had 208 galleys (including *lanternas*) at Lepanto, giving them parity in numbers. In addition they were supported by 56 *galiots* and 64 *fusta*. Although the Turks had a higher number of *bastardas* than the Christians, they had fewer *lanternas*. Like the ordinary galleys in the Christian fleet, each Turkish galley needed a *ciurma* of approximately 200 men, while the *galiots* carried about 80 men each, and the *fustas* 60. This gives an approximate fleet total of 50,000 oarsmen and sailors. 27,000 soldiers were distributed throughout the fleet, including 10,000 *Janissaries* from Greek garrisons, 2,000 dismounted *Spahis*, and approximately 4,000 volunteers and adventurers. If we assume just over 5,000 soldiers were distributed throughout the smaller *galiots* and *fustas* (with an average of 55 and 25 soldiers on each craft respectively), then about 100–120 Turkish soldiers were carried on board each galley, with proportionately more on the Turkish *lanternas*. Ali Pasha's *Sultana* (fleet *lanterna*) carried 200 *Janissaries* on board. While both sides included reliable troops, the Spanish foot and the *Janissaries* were some of the best soldiers in Europe. The fight was going to be a tough one.

Although the two fleets were relatively well matched, the Christians had the greater number of heavy ordnance, as over half the fleet carried five guns as a bow armament, an armament level which was only matched on the largest of the Turkish galleys and *lanternas*. The ordinary Venetian galleys and probably all the Turkish ones carried three bow guns. Although the numbers of soldiers were relatively equal (with a slight numerical advantage in the Christian fleet), most of these Christian soldiers were armed with arquebuses (and a few with muskets), while over two-thirds of the Turkish troops were armed with bow instead of arquebus. While the bow could maintain a higher rate of fire, its range and penetrative power was less than that of the arquebus. Other soldiers carried boarding weapons (half-pikes, swords, axes or halberds). One other advantage lay in the oarsmen. The Venetians were for the most part free men, while all other galleys were crewed by slaves, chained to the oars. The Venetians could therefore rely on their *ciurma* to participate in boarding actions, and all were armed with boarding weapons.

Although a straight comparison of numbers gives the Turks an advantage in size of fleet and the Christians in soldiery or free oarsmen, this was only part of the equation. The Turks had enough small craft to ensure they could easily reinforce any part of the line, to apply pressure in an attempt to break the enemy, or to shore up threatened sectors of the line. Even more important, the Turks enjoyed a reputation as being the most formidable fighters of the Mediterranean. Despite a handful of setbacks, they had swept all before them, and they were the terror of Europe. Rather like the Japanese during the first 18 months of the Pacific War, they enjoyed a reputation for being invincible foes. Lepanto would end this myth of invincibility.

Turning to the composition of the fleets themselves, all contemporary accounts vary slightly by up to a dozen vessels per side. To the naval commanders of the 16th century Mediterranean, the galley was expendable, while its crew and armament were not. Some Venetian galleys were condemned before the battle, and their crews transferred, while it is almost certain that several unseaworthy Turkish craft were left behind when the fleet sailed to give battle. The exact number of vessels in their fleet varied from day to day, and even the commanders on both sides were probably unaware of the exact number of galleys and men they commanded on the day of the battle. The following order of battle therefore represents an educated guess, not a definitive listing.

Marc Antonio Colonna (1535–84), the Grand Constable of Naples was a veteran Spanish commander, but lacked naval experience. Despite this he was nominated as the deputy commander of the Fleet of the Holy League, and named the commander of the Papal Contingent during the campaign. (Galleria Colonna, Rome)

ORDERS OF BATTLE

The lists given below are compiled from a combination of several sources. For the Fleet of the Holy League, the principal source has been a record in the Vatican Archive (175–180), reprinted in the study by José Aparici (Madrid, 1847). This has been cross-referenced with the ship list compiled for Don John of Austria for the 1572 campaign (i.e. after Lepanto), a copy of which is lodged in the Spanish archive at Simancas Castle, near Valladolid (*legajo* 1134). The similarity between the two lists (there are only one or two discrepancies) suggests that they are fairly accurate. Both lists were reproduced in Martinez (1972).

Another detailed and near-contemporary order of battle is provided in John Poleman's *The Second Booke of Battailes Fought in our Age* (London, 1587), drawn from an earlier Venetian list compiled by Gio. Pietro Contarini (who worked for the Arsenal of Venice). The Contarini list was first printed as part of a celebratory work in 1572, and has been reprinted in various forms during the intervening centuries. The close correlation between the two lists suggests that Poleman based his exclusively on Contarini's list, although there are slight discrepancies between the two lists. Presumably these arose during Poleman's transcription of the Venetian list.

The historian John Guilmartin Jr. drew on the Simancas list for his research, and I have followed his lead, augmenting this where appropriate with additional information supplied by Martinez.

As for the Turkish fleet, both Poleman and Contarini supplied a Christian version of the list, presumably based on records made after the battle by the Christians. This correlates reasonably closely with a tally of Turkish galley numbers given in the Vatican papers. Given the transcription errors described above, the Contarini list is probably the more accurate, and the ship numbers given tally reasonably well with those in the Vatican numeric tally. No extant Christian list provides names for the Turkish galleys, but lists them according to commander and squadron. Neither can be seen as more than passably accurate.

A similar list based on the names of the various Turkish galley commanders resides in the Topkapi Museum Archive in Istanbul, but it is incomplete, and conversations with historians working in this area have cast doubts as to both the date of its compilation and indeed to its relevance. It might refer to the fleet as it existed in 1570, not 1571, due to quirks in the Ottoman record-keeping process.

Therefore, while the order of battle provided for the Holy League can be seen as being reasonably accurate, the Turkish Order of Battle will inevitably contain errors, due to the potential inaccuracy of the sources used. More research needs to be undertaken on the Turkish order of battle, but what is presented here represents the current state of research, based on a comparison and indeed a compilation of the

Don Álvaro de Bazán (1526–88), the Marqués de Santa Cruz, was one of Spain's most renowned naval commanders. He led the Christian rearguard at Lepanto, and went on to command Spanish armadas in the Atlantic during campaigns against the French. (Museo Navale, Madrid)

extant sources. For the sake of consistency, I have followed the fleet size given by Guilmartin, and used the Istanbul list for the basic framework. The only variance with the Guilmartin list concerns the *galiot* squadron attached to the centre, which I consider was confused with elements of the Turkish reserve. In areas where information was unavailable or incomplete, I have augmented it with the rather more suspect Contarini list. In these cases, the original spelling of the commander's name as listed by Contarini in his 1572 edition has been retained, as any attempt to interpret it could create a pyramid of error.

In both fleets, all lists (contemporary or based on later research) can vary by one or two ships in each wing. By following the numerical strengths listed by Guilmartin (2002), I have attempted to remain in step with current research in this field.

THE FLEET OF THE HOLY LEAGUE [1]

THE LEFT WING – AGOSTIN BARBARIGO
(53 galleys, 2 galleasses)

Venetian Galleasses (2)
Galleass of Ambrogio Bragadino
Galleass of Antonio Bragadino

Venetian Galleys (39)
The *Lanterna* of Venice (L) – Agostino Barbarigo
The *Capitana* of Venice (L) – Marco Querini
The *Fortune* of Venice
The *Three Hands* of Venice
The *Two Dolphins* of Candia
The *Lion and Phoenix* of Candia
The *Madonna* of Candia
The *Seahorse* of Candia
The *Twin Lions* of Candia
The *Lion* of Candia
The *Christ* of Candia (I)
The *Angel* of Candia
The *Pyramid* of Candia
The *Resurrected Christ* of Venice (I)
The *Resurrected Christ* of Venice (II)
The *Christ* of Corfu
The *Resurrected Christ* of Candia (I)
The *Christ* of Venice (I)
The *Christ* of Candia (II)
The *Resurrected Christ* of Candia (II)
The *Kodus* of Candia
Santa Euphemia of Brescia
The *Blessed* of Candia
The *Seahorse* of Venice
The *Christ* of Candia (III)
The *Arm* of Candia
Our Lady of Zante
The *Resurrected Christ* of Candia (III)
Our Lady of Venice (I)
God the Father, over the Holy Trinity of Venice
The *Resurrected Christ* of Venice (III)
The *Angel* of Venice
Santa Dorothea of Venice
The *Ketianana* of Retimo
The *Lion's Head* of Istria
The *Cross* of Cephalonia
The *Virgin Saint* of Cephalonia
The *Resurrected Christ* of Vegia
San Nicolo of Cherso

Spanish and Neapolitan Galleys (12)
The *Lomellina* (Spanish) (L)
The *Flame* of Naples
San Giovanni of Naples
The *Envy* of Naples
The *Blessed* of Naples
San Jacopo of Naples
San Nicolo of Naples
The *Victory* of Naples
The *Fortune* of St. Andrew
+3 more unnamed Spanish or Neapolitan galleys

Papal Galleys (1)
Reign (Papal)

Genoese Galley (1)
The *Marchessa* of Doria

THE CENTRAL DIVISION – DON JOHN OF AUSTRIA (62 galleys, 2 galleasses)

Venetian Galleasses (2)
Galleass of Jacopo Guoro
Galleass of Francesco Duodo

Venetian Galleys (29)
The *Capitana* of Venice (L) – Sebastian Venier
The *Capitana* of Lomelini (L) – Paolo Orsini
The *Padrona* of Lomelini – Pier Battista Lomellini
The *Capitana* of Man – Giorgio d'Asti
San Giovanni of Venice
The *Tree Trunk* of Venice
The *Mongibello* of Venice
The *Virgin* of Candia
Our Lady of Venice (II)
The *Christ* of Venice (II)
The *Wheel of the Serpent*
The *Pyramid* of Venice
The *Palm* of Venice
The *San Theodoro* of Venice
The *Mountain* of Candia
San Giovanni Battista (St John the Baptist)
The *Christ* of Venice (III)
San Giovanni of Venice
The *Passaro* of Venice
The *Lion* of Venice
San Girolamo of Venice
The *Judith* of Zante
San Christoforo of Venice
The *Armelino* of Candia
The *Middle Moon* of Venice
The *Man of the Sea* of Vicenza
St Alessandro of Bergamo
San Girolamo of Lesina
+1 more unnamed Venetian galley

Genoese Galleys (8)
The *Capitana* of Genoa (L) – Ettor Spinola
The *Capitana* of Gil d'Andrada (L) – Bernardo Cinoguera
The *Padrona* of Genoa (L) – Pellerano
The *Padrona* of David Imperiali – Nicolo da Luvano
The *Pearl* (Andrea Doria)
The *Temperance*
The *Victory* (Andrea Doria)
The *Pyramid* (Andrea Doria)

Spanish and Neapolitan Galleys (16)
The *Real* (Spanish) (L) – Don John of Austria (flagship)
The *Capitana* of Castille (Spanish) (L) – Master of Requesens
The *Capitana* of Savoy (Savoyard) (L) – Prince of Urbino, Admiral of Savoy

The *Padrona Real* (Spanish) (L) – Master Requisens
The *Capitana* of Bandinella (Neapolitan) (L) – Bendinelli Sauli
The *Capitana* of Grimaldi (Neapolitan) (L) – Georgio Grimaldi
The *Padrona* of Naples (L) – Francesco de Bonavides
The *Fortress* of Spain
San Francisco of Spain
The *Granata* of Spain
The *Figiera* of Spain
The *Moon* of Spain
The *Fortune* of Naples
The *Mendozza* of Naples
The *St George* of Naples
+1 more unnamed Spanish or Neapolitan galley

Papal Galleys (6) (including Tuscan contingent)
The *Capitana* of His Holiness (L) – Marco Antonio Colonna (Papal Flagship)
Tuscany (Tuscany)
Pisa (Tuscany)
Florence (Tuscany)
Peace
Victory

Galleys (Knights of Malta) (3)
The *Capitana* of Malta – Justin, The Prior of Messina (Maltese Flagship)
The Order of St Peter
The Order of St John

THE RIGHT WING – GIAN ANDREA DORIA
(53 galleys, 2 galleasses)

Venetian Galleasses (2)
Galleass of Andrea da Cesaro
Galleass of Pietro Pisani

Venetian Galleys (25)
The *Padrona* of Mani (Parini) – Antonio Corniglia
The *Forces* of Venice
The *Rema* of Candia
The *Nino* of Venice
The *Resurrected Christ* of Venice (IV)
The *Palm* of Candia
The *Angel* of Corfu
The *Ship* of Venice
Our Lady of Candia
Christ of Candia (IV)
The *Flame* of Candia
The *Eagle* of Candia
San Cristoforo of Venice
The *Christ* of Venice (IV)
The *Hope* of Candia
The *San Giuseppe* of Venice
The *Tower* of Vicenza
The *Eagle* of Corfu
The *Eagle* of Retimo
The *San Giovanni* of Arbe
The *Lady* of Friuli (Trau)
The *Reality* of Padua
+3 more unnamed Venetian galleys

Spanish and Neapolitan Galleys (10)
The *Sicilian*
The *Piedmont* (Savoyard)
The *Margaret* of Savoy (Savoyard)
The *Cingana* of Naples
The *Moon* of Naples
The *Hope* of Naples
The *Gusmana* of Naples
+3 more unnamed Spanish or Neapolitan galleys

Genoese Galleys (16)
The *Capitana* of Andrea Doria (L) – Andrea Doria
The *Capitana* of Negroni (L) – Giovan Ambrogio
  Negroni
The *Padrona* of Grimaldi – Lorenzo Trecha
The *Padrona* of Andrea Doria (L) – Giulio Centurioni
The *Padrona* of Negroni (L) – Luigi Gamba
The *Padrona* of Lomellini – Georgio Greco
The *Swordsman* of Retimo
San Vittorio of Crema
The *Fury* of Lomellini
The *Negrona*
The *Bastard* of Negrona
The *San Tritone* of Cataro
The *Monarch* of Giovan Andrea
The *Maid* of Giovan Andrea
The *Diana* of Genoa
+1 more unnamed Genoese galley

Papal Galleys (2)
Sta Maria
San Giovanni

THE REARGUARD – DON ÁLVARO DE BAZÁN
(38 galleys, including 8 galleys of the Advanced Guard)

Venetian Galleys (12)
The *Christ* of Venice
The *Two Hands* of Venice
The *Faith* of Venice
The *Pillar* of Venice
The *Magdalene* of Venice
The *Lady* of Venice
The *World* of Venice
The *Hope* of Venice
San Pietro of Venice
The *Sybil* of Venice
San Giorgio of Sebenico
San Michele

Spanish and Neapolitan Galleys (13)
The *Capitana* of Naples (L) – Don Álvaro de Bazán,
  Marquis de Santa Cruz
The *Capitana* of Vaicos (Spanish) (L) – Vasquez de
  Coronado
San Giovanni of Sicily (Spanish)
The *Crane* (Spanish)
The *Leona* of Naples
The *Constanza* of Naples
The *Marcheza* of Naples
The *Sta Barbara* of Naples
The *San Andrea* of Naples
The *Santa Caterina* of Naples
The *San Angelo* of Naples
The *Terana* of Naples
+1 more unnamed Spanish or Neapolitan galley

Papal Galleys (3)
The *Padrona* of the Papacy (L) – Alfonso d'Appiano
Supremacy
Serenity

Genoese Galleys (2)
The *Baccana* of Genoa
+1 more unnamed Genoese galley

THE VANGUARD – GIOVANNI DI CARDONA
(8 galleys. Attached to the Reserve)

The *Capitana* of Sicily (Spanish) – Giovanni di Cardona
The *Padrona* of Sicily (Spanish)
San Giovanni of Sicily (Spanish)
San Ionica of Sicily (Spanish)
Santa Magdalena of Venice
The *Sun* of Venice
St Catherine of Venice
Our Woman of Venice

THE TURKISH FLEET [2]

THE LEFT WING – ULUCH ALI
(61 galleys, 32 galiots)

Turkish (Constantinople) Galleys (14)
Nasur Ferhad (L)
Kasam Rais (L)
Osman Rais (L)
Kiafi Hajji
Ferhad Ali
Memi Bey
Piri Osman
Piri Rais
Salan Basti
Talatagi Rais
Celebi Rais
Tartar Ali
Kiafir Hajji
Karaman Pasha

Barbary (Algerian) Galleys (14)
Uluch Ali (L) – wing commander
Kari Ali (L)
Karaman Ali
Alemdar Pasha
Sinian Celebi
Amdjazade Mustafa
Dragud Ali
Seydi Ali
Peri Selim
Murad Darius
Uluj Rais
Macazir Ali
Ionas Osman
Salim Deli

Syrian Galleys (6)
Kara Bey (L)
Dermat Bey
Osman Beyt
Iusuf Ali
Kari Alemdar
Murad Hasan

Anatolian Galleys (13)
Karali Rais (L)
Piriman Rais (L)
Hazull Sinian
Chios Mehemet
Hignau Mustafa
Cademly Mustafa
Uschiufly Memy
Kari Mora
Darius Pasha
Piali Osman
Tursun Osman
Iosul Piali
Keduk Seydi

Greek (Negropont) Galleys (14)
Seydi Rais (L)
Arnaud Ali (L)
Chendereli Mustafa
Mustafa Hajji
Sali Rais
Hamid Ali
Karaman Hyder
Magyar Fehrad
Nasuh Ferhad
Nasi Rais
Kara Rhodi
Kos Hajji
Kos Memi
Karam Bey (Albanian)

Turkish (Constantinople) Galiots (19)
Uluj Piri Pasha (L)
Karaman Suleiman
Haneshi Ahmed
Hyder Enver
Nur Memi
Karaman Rais
Kalaman Memi
Guzman Ferhad
Hunyadis Hasan
Kemal Murad
Sarmusai Rais

Tursun Suleiman
Celebi Iusuf
Hasedi Hasan
Sian Memi
Osman Bagli
Karaman Rais
+2 more unnamed Turkish galiots

Albanian Galiots (8)
Deli Murad
Alemdar Rais
Sian Siander
Alemdar Rais
Hasan Omar
Seydi Aga
Hasan Sinam
Jami Fazil

Anatolian Galiots (5)
Kara Alemdhar
Suzi Memi
Nabi Rais
Hasan Osman
Hunyadi Iusuf

THE CENTRE – ALI PASHA (87 galleys) [3]

FIRST LINE (62 galleys)

Turkish (Constantinople) Galleys (22)
Muezzenade Ali Pasha *Sultana* (L) – Fleet flagship
Osman Rais (L) – wing commander
Portasi Pasha (L) – commander, embarked troops
Hasan Pasha (son of Barbarossa) (L)
Hasan Rais
Kos Ali
Kilik Rais
Uluj Rais
Piri Uluj Bey
Dardagan Rais – Governor of the Arsenal
Deli Osman
Piri Osman
Demir Celebi
Darius Haseki
Sinian Mustafa
Haseki Rais
Hasan Uluj
Kosem Iusuf
Aga Ahmed
Osman Seydi
Darius Celebi
Kafar Rais

Rhodes Galleys (12)
Hasan Bey – Governor of Rhodes (L)
Deli Chender – Warden of Rhodes (L)
Osa Rais
Postana Uluj
Khalifa Uluj
Ghazni Rais
Dromus Rais
Berber Kali
Karagi Rais
Occan Rais
Deli Ali
Hajji Aga

Black Sea (Bulgarian and Bithynian) Galleys (13)
Preuil Aga (L)
Kara Rais (L)
Arnaud Rais
Jami Uluj
Arnaua Celebi
Magyar Ali
Kafi Celebi
Deli Celebi
Deli Assan
Karaperi Aga
Sinian Rais
Kari Mustafa
Seydi Arnaud

Gallipoli Galleys (4)
The *Lord* of Moria (L)
Piri Hamagi
Ali Rais
Iusuf Ali
Sinian Bektashi

24

Greek (Negropont) Galleys (11)
Osman Rais (L)
Mehmed Bey – Governor of Metelina (L)
Baktashi Uluj
Baktashi Mustafa
Sinian Ali
Agdagi Rais
Deli Iusuf
Orphan Ali
Kali Celebi
Bagdar Rais
Hanyadi Mustafa

SECOND LINE (25 galleys, 8 galiots)

Constantinople Galleys (12)
Tramontana Rais (L)
Murad Rais
Suleiman Celebi
Deli Ibraim
Murad Korosi
Damad Ali
Kari Rais
Darius Sinian
Dardagi Ali
Hyder Carai
Darius Ali
Kari Ali

Barbary (Tripoli) Galleys (6)
Hyder Aga
Kari Hamat
Husan Kalim Ali
Daram Uluj
Seydi Ali
Mohammed Ali

Gallipoli Galleys (7)
Azizs Khalifa – Governor of Gallipoli (L)
Selim Sahi
Seydi Pasha
Hasan Mustafa
Haseri Ali
Haseri Deli
Iusuf Seydi

RIGHT WING – MEHMET SULIK PASHA
(60 galleys, 2 galiots)

Turkish (Constantinople) Galleys (20)
Suleiman Bey (L)
Kara Mustafa (L)
Ibrahim Rais
Suleiman Rais
Karaman Ibrahim
Chender Sinian
Hasan Nabi
Ali 'Genoese'
Halil Rais
Seydi Selim
Kumar Iusuf
Bardas Celebi
Bardas Hasan
Fazil Ali Bey
Drusali Piri
Koda Ali
Sinaman Mustafa
Caracoza Ali
Mustafa Alendi
Marmara Rais

Barbary (Tripoli) Galleys (5)
Arga Pasha (L)
Arnaut Ferhad
Damad Iusuf
Suleiman Rais
Fazil Memi

Anatolian Galleys (13)
Mehemet Bey – *Capitana*
Mysor Ali
Amurat Rais
Kalifi Memi
Murad Mustafa
Hyder Mehmet
Sinian Darius
Mehmet Darius
Amdjazade Sinian

Adagi Hasan
Sinjji Musafa
Hajji Cebebi
Tursan Mustafa

Egyptian (Alexandrian) Galleys (22)
Mehmet Sulik Pasha (L) – wing commander
Kari Ali (L)
Herus Rais (L)
Karas Turbat
Bagli Sarif
Hasan Celebi
Osman Celebi
Dink Kasali
Osman Occan
Darius Aga
Drazed Sinian
Osman Ali
Deli Aga
Dardagut Bardabey
Kasli Khan
Iusuf Aga
Iusuf Magyar
Khalifa Hyder
Mustafa Kemal
Damadi Piri
Memi Hasan
Kari Ali

Egyptian (Alexandrian) Galiots (2)
Abdul Rais
Piali Murad

THE REARGUARD – AMURAT DRAGUT RAIS
(8 galleys, 22 galiots)[4]

Greek (Negropont) Galleys (4)
Amurat Dragut Rais
Kaidar Memi
Deli Dori
Hasan Sinian

Anatolian Galleys (4)
Deli Suleiman
Deli Bey
Kiafar Bey
Kasim Sinian

Mixed Squadron of Galiots (22)
Ali Uluj
Kara Deli
Ferhad Kara Ali
Dardagud Rais
Kasim Kara
Hasan Rais
Alemdar Hasan
Kos Ali
Hajji Ali
Kurtoprulu Celebi
Setagi Memi
Setagi Osman
Hyder Ali
Hyder Deli
Armad Memi
Hasan Rais
Jami Naser
Nur Ali
Kari Ali Rais
Murad Ali
Iumez Ali
Haneschi Murad

NOTES

1 Where appropriate, the vessel names have been Anglicised. Also, several vessels bore the same name. This did not seem to bother the Christian commanders, but presumably within their own national contingent, similarly named galleys were differentiated by adding the name of the commander (e.g. Giovanni Cornaro's *Christ* of Candia, Andrea Cornaro's *Christ* of Candia, Francesco Cornaro's *Christ* of Candia or Daniel Calafati's *Christ* of Candia). To simplify matters, I have elected to identify them by name and number (e.g. *Christ* of Candia I, *Christ* of Candia II etc.). An 'L' after a vessels name signifies that it was a *lanterna*.

2 Contemporary Turkish records referred to individual galleys by the name of their commander rather than by the name of the ship itself. Therefore, unlike the Christian fleet, no individual ship names are known or, at least, have been unearthed. Rather, the relevant galley was listed by its commander, and then grouped according to its squadron. For the sake of simplicity, the term *lanterna* has been used to refer to large flagship galleys, and *Sultana* for the fleet flagship of Müezzenade Ali Pasha.

3 An additional squadron of 8 galiots was listed as being attached to the Turkish centre, but the commanders of the vessels are unnamed. There is a strong possibility this unit was included amongst the 22 galiots of the reserve, or was confused with the 8 galleys attached to the reserve. To avoid confusion I have omitted them from the order of battle.

4 In addition 64 *fustas* were attached to the reserve. These small oared vessels were used to transfer reinforcements from one portion of the line to the other. It is unclear whether they were concentrated behind the central 'Battle' or not, but it is likely they were apportioned throughout the fleet, supporting the galleys of the left and right wings as well as the centre.

King Philip II of Spain (1527–1600) was the most powerful monarch in Europe, and despite the division of his father's empire when Philip succeeded him in 1556, he remained the de facto head of a Habsburg 'superpower', incorporating both the Spanish Empire and Germany. (Glasgow Museums and Art Galleries)

25

OPPOSING PLANS

THE CHRISTIAN FLEET

On 3 October 1571 the Venetian scout Gil d'Andrada rejoined the Fleet of the Holy League off Corfu, bringing news that Greek informants considered the Turkish fleet to be inferior in both men and galleys. Don John decided to seek out the enemy. A council of war was held, and Don John and his three advisers arranged the fleet in its battle formation. It was split into two wings of approximately equal size, flanking a central 'Battle' that was slightly larger than the flanking formations. It was considered unlikely that the Turks would venture far from Lepanto, so it was expected that any forthcoming battle would take place in the relatively confined waters of the Gulf of Patras, or the Gulf of Corinth. The Venetian contingent was short of men, despite Spanish and Italian soldiers having been drafted into the Venetian galleys to make up numbers. The vanguard was composed primarily of Venetian galleys, as they were faster and more manoeuvrable than their Spanish or Genoese counterparts. Elsewhere, the Venetians were divided throughout the fleet. In addition, Don John created a rearguard of 30 vessels, and a small scouting advanced guard of eight fast galleys. Allocating positions to contingents within each 'Battle' was a diplomatic headache for the Christian commander. The Knights of Malta were reluctant to station themselves in their allotted place in the central 'Battle' due to a disagreement with the Savoyard contingent commander, who was adjacent in the line. The Venetians refused to serve under any Genoese commander, until diplomatic wrangling led to a

The *lanterna* or flagship galley of a fleet contingent was a vessel that pushed the envelope of oared warship technology to the limits. Each oar was powered by up to eight oarsmen, and a devastating bow armament was augmented by a large contingent of arquebusiers, musketeers and swordsmen. From Furttenbach's 'Architectura Navalis', 1629. (Stratford Archive)

RIGHT **A colourful depiction of a Muslim galley from the Barbary Coast. Although relatively lightly equipped with ordnance and soldiers, these craft were usually lighter and faster than other galleys of the period. (Stratford Archive)**

A Turkish galley at anchor. Turkish galleys were of a similar size to their Christian counterparts, they tended to rely less on a powerful armament of bow guns than other galleys, and relied more on speed and manoeuvrability under oars. (Topkapi Sarayi Muzei, Istanbul)

grudging acceptance of temporary attachment to Andrea Doria's 'Battle'. Finally the six available *galleasses* were split between the three 'Battles'. The general plan was for the fleet to form up in a similar fashion to contemporary armies, with the vanguard, main body and rearguard in line abreast. In the rear the reserve would form up behind the main or centre body. The *galleasses* would then row or be towed into place in front of the three 'Battles', where they would act as a 'forlorn hope', charged with disrupting the enemy fleet before it came into contact with the main Christian line. This line abreast formation was designed to make maximum use of the fleet's artillery. As reports indicated that the Turkish fleet was smaller than that of the Holy League, Don John expected to deploy approximately 200 more pieces of ordnance in his front line than the enemy.

As the fleet rowed southwards towards Cephalonia and the mouth of the Gulf of Patras, Don John completed his arrangements. Nightly halts and fog gave him plenty of time to contemplate his deployment, and a second council of war was held at dawn on 6 October. Although it was expected to encounter the Turkish fleet at some stage over the following week, a lack of hard information made detailed planning difficult. Some commanders favoured raiding Turkish towns along the Adriatic shore, but the Venetians refused to contemplate a division of effort. They feared that the Turks could attack while the fleet was distracted and when men were busy on shore. Fresh information reported that Uluch Ali and a portion of the Turkish fleet had left Lepanto and were at sea somewhere in the Gulf of Corinth. It was still considered unlikely that battle was imminent, but Don John insisted that the crews remain vigilant and prepared for action as they approached the entrance to the Gulf. His vigilance was rewarded, as the Turks were further west than anyone realised. A forward base was selected at Porta Petala, just north of the Gulf, and from there it was expected that the fleet would reconnoitre cautiously along the Gulf's northern shore, in an attempt to locate the enemy fleet. Most expected that, as the Turks were reported to be outnumbered, they would withdraw behind the guns and fortifications of Lepanto, rather

The Venetian *galleass* was not a true hybrid between galley and sailing 'roundship', but its design permitted the use of a small broadside armament. The bulk of its compliment of guns was mounted in the circular fortress-like forecastle. Copy of an engraving by Bertelli, dated 1573. (Stratford Archive)

than risk battle against a superior enemy. As a final precaution, Don John ordered that all galley captains should saw off the ram and beak (*spiron*) on their vessels, to give their bow guns a better field of fire, and allow them to depress to fire on ships in bow-to-bow contact with them. Nothing could provide a clearer demonstration of the Christian superiority in artillery and their faith in their guns than this order. He expected to anchor his fleet off Scropha Point the following day, while his advanced guard probed into the Gulf of Patras. Fortunately for Don John, when dawn broke and his leading ships spotted the entire Turkish fleet heading towards them down the Gulf of Patras, the Christian fleet was as ready as it could be for the coming battle.

A *fusta* was a smaller version of a full-sized galley, and was primarily used for reconnaissance, the carrying of dispatches, and the transfer of reinforcements behind the main galley line during a battle. In this sketch, based on a watercolour by Raphael, the crew are shown taking in their lateen sail. (Stratford Archive)

THE TURKISH FLEET

Uluch Ali thought he knew the size of the Christian fleet. Scouting *galiots*, which had probed as far north as Corfu, reported that Don John commanded about 140 galleys. This underestimation would prove a costly mistake. It is likely that the Barbary Corsair who commanded the scouting expedition failed to spot Andrea Doria's rearguard, which always anchored well astern of the rest of the fleet each night, to avoid any potential conflict with the main Venetian commanders. Two batches of reinforcements had brought the Turkish fleet up to strength, making up for losses incurred through sickness over the previous two months. These included 12,000 elite *Janissaries* and *Spahis* culled from Turkish garrisons in Greece.

On 4 October scouts brought news that the Christians had set sail the day before and were heading south. A council of war was held in the castle at Lepanto. Ali Pasha read his orders from the Grand Vizier, ordering him to fight the enemy wherever possible. Young commanders such as Hassan, the son of Barbarossa, were in favour of an immediate attack. Uluch Ali supported this view, adding that the fleet should not remain in port 'playing with the women' of Lepanto. Not surprisingly, when he returned to Constantinople after the battle, he claimed to have urged caution, a claim that was refuted by reports from Turkish prisoners. Mehmet Sulik Pasha ('Sirocco') and Mehemet, Bey of Negropont, advocated caution,

This detail from a fresco depicting a Spanish amphibious landing at Terciera in the Azores in 1582 provides us with a good impression of how galleys were used in support of shore operations during this period. Unlike sailing warships, galleys remained operationally and even tactically tied to the land. (Palace of the Marquis de Santa Cruz, Viso del Marques, La Mancha).

In this detail of a gunnery diagram of the late 16th century, a galley is shown mounting a single large bombard on its centreline. By the time of Lepanto far larger suites of ordnance were the norm. From Tartaglias 'Book of Colloquies', 1588. (Stratford Archive)

requesting fresh scouting reports, as the rashness of the Christian advance suggested they considered themselves to be strong enough to offer battle. 'Sirocco' seemed to be the only senior commander who questioned the scouting reports of Caracoggia, whose *galiots* were busy probing between Cephalonia and Corfu. He added that the season was well advanced, and the Christian fleet would be short of supplies, and would have to retire within a month, leaving the Turks in control of the Morean coast. He also questioned just how difficult it would be controlling the Christian galley slaves in the fight. Pertau Pasha, commanding the embarked soldiers, agreed with 'Sirocco'.

After hearing the arguments, Ali Pasha re-read his orders, adding that he considered it unlikely that the Christians would offer battle, and were unlikely to advance beyond Cephalonia until their sailing supply squadron

Even as late as 1571 the Turks still relied on archers more than firearm-equipped soldiers in their galley fleets. Detail from a Venetian coloured engraving depicting the battle of Zonchio, 1499. (British Museum, London)

joined them. Finally, he reported the results of the interrogation of captured prisoners, who spoke of dissent in the Christian ranks, and friction between the Venetians and the Spanish. Ali Pasha made his decision. The fleet would sail west towards Cephalonia, then if the Christians retired, he would follow them, land troops on Corfu and besiege the island's fortress during the winter. With Corfu in Turkish hands, his fleet could raid as far as Venice the following spring. If the Christians decided to fight, he would be ready for them.

Like his Christian counterpart, Ali Pasha divided his fleet into three 'battles', consisting of a large centre, flanked by two slightly smaller wings. Unlike the Christians, he split his centre into two lines, so that one could reinforce the other once it came into contact with the enemy. A rearguard would stand by to reinforce the wings using light galleys (*galiots* or *fustas*) as required. He expected his infantrymen to have the edge in combat, particularly as his centre included the veteran *Janissaries*, supported by local troops and archers. At dawn on 6 October the fleet left Lepanto and rowed east in light winds, anchoring for the night off Galata, on the northern shore of the Gulf of Patras. Fresh reinforcements were brought aboard, but if Ali Pasha made any last-minute adjustments to his dispositions, the changes were never recorded. Caracoggia and his scouts arrived during the night, reporting that the Christian fleet was off Ithaca and was expected to continue on towards Cephalonia in the morning. Therefore, unlike the Christians, the Turks were aware that a battle was imminent. The fleet sailed before dawn, ready and eager for the coming fight...

THE CAMPAIGN

THE END OF AN ERA

Several historians have seen the Siege of Malta in 1565 as the high-water mark of Ottoman Turkish expansion. From that point on, the Turks lapsed into a period marked by decadence, strategic indifference and court intrigue that brought about a steady decline of Turkish military abilities and ambitions. In fact, the Turks remained very much on the offensive for a decade after the Siege of Malta was abandoned, and a more accurate milestone was the death of the man who had masterminded Turkish expansion for almost half a century.

On 8 September 1566, the Turkish army of Sultan Süleyman I 'the Magnificent' captured the small Hungarian town of Szigeth (Szigetvar), a key fortress on the road from Belgrade to Vienna. Unknown to his soldiers, the Great Sultan, ruler of 37 kingdoms, had actually died two days before. Still seen as a colossus who dominated the European stage, by 1566 Süleyman 'the Magnificent' was 72, plagued by illness and probably suffering from bouts of senility. Although he still led his armies in person (and had done since 1521), much of his power was vested in the hands of his Grand Vizier, Sokullu Mehmed Pasha. It was Sokullu who had declared war on the Holy Roman Empire in January 1566, probably as a means of regaining the initiative in Europe after the debacle at Malta the previous year. It was also the Vizier who kept the news of the Sultan's death from his army, lest the troops lose heart. The secret of the death of the Great Sultan was kept for another two weeks while messengers rushed to Constantinople, allowing the Sultan's only surviving son, Selim, to secure his succession.

The Szigeth campaign was both the last of 13 military campaigns in the Danube Valley led by Süleyman 'the Magnificent' and the last threat to Christian Europe posed by a Turkish army. Although other invasions would follow (most notably the attack on Vienna in 1683), none had any real chance of achieving success, and posed little threat to the stability of Europe. The death of Süleyman marked the end of an era, therefore. Although Turkish military expansion would continue for several more years, without dynamic leadership, the Turkish army was no longer a force to be reckoned with in central Europe. The situation in the Mediterranean was different, as the Turks still had a powerful fleet, extensive resources, and a handful of dynamic naval commanders.

Süleyman was succeeded by his son Selim II 'the Sot', who reigned from 1566 to 1575. Brought up in an atmosphere of court intrigue, Selim had seen his brothers executed one after the other by his father, the Great Sultan. To escape from this threatening atmosphere, Prince Selim took to drink, a vice which he pursued unchecked once he gained the throne. Like his father during his final years, Sultan Selim relied on

An Ottoman Turkish army on the march, with *Janissaries* forming the central column. During the Lepanto campaign the Turks augmented their fleet by reinforcing it with professional soldiers from the Greek garrisons. These troops included elite *Janissaries*. (Topkapi Sarayi Muzei, Istanbul)

A German gun foundry during the late 16th century. The increasing availability of high-quality bronze ordnance to both Christian and Muslim governments meant that galleys were becoming increasingly well armed as the century progressed. (Author's Collection)

Spanish officers of the Lepanto period, shown wearing Spanish-styled morion helmets and breastplates or quilted doublets. By this period the Spanish soldiers in the fleet were amongst the best trained, equipped and led in the Mediterranean. Detail from a garden fresco. (Palace of the Marquis de Santa Cruz, Viso del Marques, La Mancha)

his Grand Vizier, Sokullu Mehmed Pasha to run his empire for him, and to dictate policy.

He inherited an empire that was at war on two fronts; in central Europe (where his troops fought the Emperor Maximilian), and in the Mediterranean, where the Turks were at war with Philip II of Spain. Unlike his father, Selim had no intention of campaigning at the head of his army. A peace treaty was signed with the Emperor Maximilian in February 1568, and the status quo on the Danube frontier was restored without any significant exchange of territory. This left the war with Spain. Since Malta, the political situation had changed in the central Mediterranean. The Spanish were temporarily distracted by a revolt amongst the *Moriscos* or Moors in southern Spain, and by the revolt against Spanish authority in the Netherlands. Both revolts were the result of the heavy-handed religious policies of the Spanish king, and tied down troops, resources and commanders. This allowed the Barbary Corsairs to launch an attack on Tunis[3], and the city was captured in 1569 (although the last Tunisian stronghold did not capitulate until early 1570). The Turkish fleet under the veteran commander Piali Pasha launched raids on the coast of southern Italy, which clearly demonstrated the absence of Spanish naval and military muscle. If Süleyman had still been on the throne, he would probably have taken advantage of the temporary distraction of Philip II and his forces. A renewed war with Spain in 1569 might have resulted in significant gains for the Turks, but instead, Selim II allowed himself to be distracted by a revolt in Arabia, and in the possibilities offered by a naval adventure closer to home.

THE CYPRUS CAMPAIGN OF 1570

Since 1540, the Republic of Venice had played no part in the 'holy war' against the Turks in the Mediterranean. For the past three decades, Venetian neutrality allowed the city's merchants to trade with the Middle East, and to maintain a string of colonial outposts in the eastern

3 Although Islamic, the rulers of Tunis had managed to resist Ottoman domination, largely as a result of military and financial backing from the Spanish Crown.

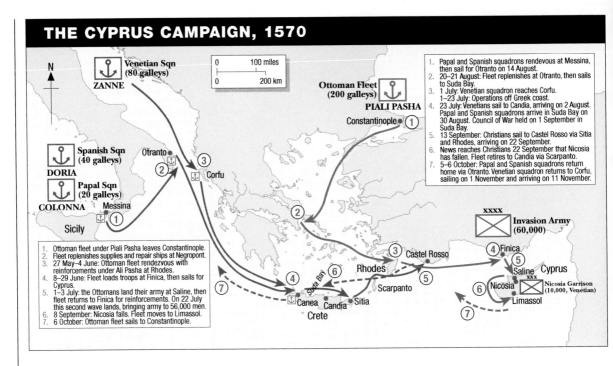

THE CYPRUS CAMPAIGN, 1570

Venetian Sqn (80 galleys)
ZANNE

Spanish Sqn (40 galleys)
DORIA

Papal Sqn (20 galleys)
COLONNA

Messina
Sicily

Otranto

Corfu

Ottoman Fleet (200 galleys)
PIALI PASHA

Constantinople

Castel Rosso
Rhodes
Scarpanto
Suda Bay
Canea Candia Sitia
Crete

XXXX Invasion Army (60,000)

Finica
Saline Cyprus
Nicosia
Limassol
Nicosia Garrison (10,000, Venetian)

1. Papal and Spanish squadrons rendevous at Messina, then sail for Otranto on 14 August.
2. 20–21 August: Fleet replenishes at Otranto, then sails to Suda Bay.
3. 1 July: Venetian squadron reaches Corfu.
   1–23 July: Operations off Greek coast.
4. 23 July: Venetians sail to Candia, arriving on 2 August. Papal and Spanish squadrons arrive in Suda Bay on 30 August. Council of War held on 1 September in Suda Bay.
5. 13 September: Christians sail to Castel Rosso via Sitia and Rhodes, arriving on 22 September.
6. News reaches Christians 22 September that Nicosia has fallen. Fleet retires to Candia via Scarpanto.
7. 5–6 October: Papal and Spanish squadrons return home via Otranto. Venetian squadron returns to Corfu, sailing on 1 November and arriving on 11 November.

1. Ottoman fleet under Piali Pasha leaves Constantinople.
2. Fleet replenishes supplies and repair ships at Negropont.
3. 27 May–4 June: Ottoman fleet rendezvous with reinforcements under Ali Pasha at Rhodes.
4. 8–29 June: Fleet loads troops at Finica, then sails for Cyprus.
5. 1–3 July: the Ottomans land their army at Saline, then fleet returns to Finica for reinforcements. On 22 July this second wave lands, bringing army to 56,000 men.
6. 8 September: Nicosia falls. Fleet moves to Limassol.
7. 6 October: Ottoman fleet sails to Constantinople.

Mediterranean. Successive civic leaders ignored Papal requests to join any 'crusade', and left the Spanish and the Papacy to continue their war against the Muslims of the Barbary Coast and the Ottoman Empire without the support of the largest Christian maritime power in the Mediterranean. The drawback with this policy was that her colonial empire was only safe from the Turks so long as the Venetians could maintain a naval supremacy in the eastern Mediterranean. Without the fleet, the Venetian-held islands of Cyprus and Crete were indefensible, as were her mainland outposts in Morea (the Peloponnese), and in the islands off the Adriatic coast of Greece. Advisers convinced the Great Sultan that the danger of intervention by Spain and the rest of the Christian maritime powers in the event of a war with Venice in the Mediterranean was negligible. Apparently, the Grand Vizier counselled against a war with Venice, but Selim was swayed by Piali Pasha, who saw an attack on Venice as a precursor to a renewed offensive in the Mediterranean. The rather fatuous suggestion that Selim 'the Sot' was swayed by the fact that Cyprus produced the best wines in the region can be ignored as Christian propaganda. In the event of a war, Piali Pasha guaranteed the ability of the Turkish fleet to gain local naval supremacy in the eastern Mediterranean, and to cut off Cyprus from aid and reinforcement. In any event, Venetian reinforcements would have to travel some 1,300 miles (2,000km) from Venice to Cyprus, while the Turks could reinforce their attacking army from major ports in Syria and Anatolia. Venetian Cyprus was out on a limb.

A great fire ravaged the naval Arsenal of Venice in late 1569, and although reports of damage to the Venetian galley fleet proved greatly exaggerated, the Turkish Sultan was encouraged by the news. All he needed was a good excuse to declare war. Selim looked to his religion for a *casus belli*. He asked the Mufti Ebn Said whether it was the duty of a Muslim ruler to recover lands that were once in Muslim hands but

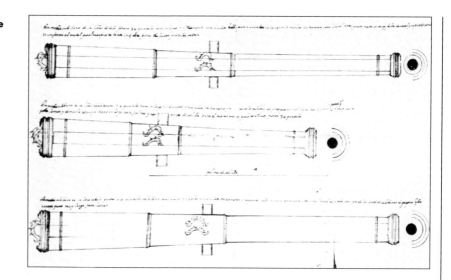

A diagram in the Spanish archive of the period underlines the variety of ordnance used on board ship, and stresses the importance of employing guns with the right combination of length, weight and bore size. (Archivas de Simancas)

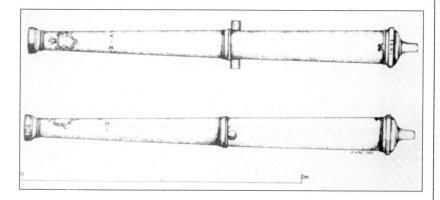

A Venetian 'sacre' (saker) of the late 17th century, cast by the Venetian founder Zigismundo Alberghetti, a member of the leading Italian family of gunfounders. The piece was recovered from a wreck off the Isle of Wight. (Author's Collection)

which had since fallen to the infidel. The Arabs had held Cyprus from AD649 to 746 after they ejected the ruling Byzantines, and again from AD826–965, after a period of Byzantine reconquest. Cyprus was recaptured by the Byzantines again in AD965, and then fell to Frankish crusaders in 1191. The island remained under its crusading Lusignan rulers until Cyprus was ceded to Venice in 1489. The Mufti answered in the affirmative, and a 'holy war' of reconquest was duly declared in February 1570.

A large Turkish invasion force was readied in Anatolia, while Piali Pasha left Constantinople with the main Turkish fleet in April. A second fleet commanded by Ali Pasha joined him at Rhodes, and together the two fleets sailed for Finica in Anatolia, where the Turkish invasion force was waiting. The Turkish general Mustapha Pasha was duly embarked, along with 56,000 troops, including a corps of 6,000 elite *Janissaries*. The Turks arrived off the northern Cypriot port of Seline on 1 July, and after protecting the disembarkation of the army, Piali Pasha led his fleet round to the southern coast of the island, where he blockaded the port of Limassol. A further 14,000 troops reinforced Mustapha Pasha's army three weeks later. There was no sign of the Venetian fleet.

Cyprus was a mountainous island kingdom that offered several defensive options to the Venetian defenders. Three years before, in 1567, the task of fortifying the Cypriot capital of Nicosia had been completed,

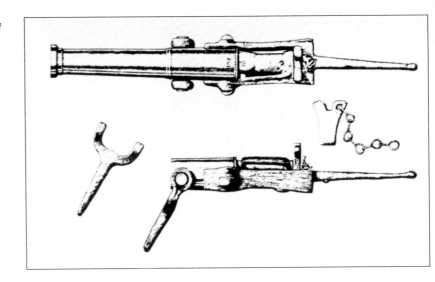

A large 'falcon pedrero', a type of pintle-mounted Spanish swivel gun, which formed part of the secondary armament of a war galley, mounted on top of the *arrumbada* (fighting platform), or around the poop deck. Pedreros were designed to fire stone projectiles. Drawing by Dr. Colin Martin. (Author's Collection)

A Spanish 'verso', the standard swivel gun of the period. It was capable of firing a small charge of musket balls, scrap metal and nails at point blank range, immediately before two galleys clashed. Recovered from the 'Maravillas Wreck', Bahamas, by the salvage company Marex Ltd. (Author's Collection)

A clay 'firepot' could be filled with an incendiary concoction akin to modern napalm, and hurled on board an enemy vessel. The pieces of matchcord strapped to the vessel were lit immediately before it was thrown. Illustration from a contemporary Spanish ordnance treatise. (Author's Collection)

and it now boasted a formidable set of modern fortifications. In theory, its network of artillery bastions, ditches and outworks should have been able to withstand any assault, buying time for a Venetian relief force to reach the island. By contrast, the medieval walls of the main port of Famagusta near the eastern tip of the island were not expected to provide much of an obstacle to a Turkish army equipped with modern artillery. Nicolo Dandolo, the Governor of Cyprus, had less than 10,000 men at his disposal and was outnumbered by about 7 to 1. This force included approximately 3,000 Venetian foot soldiers, 4,000 Cypriot militia, 1,500 Italian mercenaries, 500 gunners, and 1,000 cavalry, the latter being the remnants of the crusading nobility who had ruled the island for two and a half centuries. Dandalo decided that it was futile to try to hold the whole island, or to block the Turks in the mountains, where his force would be cut off from any reinforcements. Instead, he elected to deploy his troops in Nicosia and Famagusta, winning time for a relief force to come to his rescue.

The Turks took two weeks to reach Nicosia, and the siege began a week later, on 22 July. This fortified jewel in the Venetian crown was expected to hold out for at least a year. Instead, Nicosia fell within seven weeks. At first the Turks tried to dig mines to breach the walls, and emplaced siege batteries around the city. The walls proved virtually impregnable, and two

A contemporary model of Don John's flagship, or *Real*. Although probably less than accurate, it provides us with some indication of the armament fitted to the vessel, both in the form of a powerful bow battery and in a series of smaller pieces mounted along the hull sides, and around the poop deck. (Museu Maritim, Barcelona)

initial assaults on outworks were repulsed. Although the defences proved sound, Dandolo had too few men to garrison them effectively, given the size of the Turkish army camped outside the city walls. Mustapha Pasha quickly realised that his best chance to capture the city lay in an assault, not in a protracted siege, or the steady reduction of the defences. A third assault was launched on 9 September, with co-ordinated secondary attacks pinning the defenders around the defensive perimeter, while the *Janissaries* launched the main assault. The Venetians were unable to defend everywhere, and once the *Janissaries* gained a foothold on the walls, Turkish reinforcements flooded into the city and overwhelmed the defenders. As the defences were breached, Dandolo and his surviving garrison retreated to the Governor's Palace, where they made a last stand. This last pocket of resistance fell by nightfall, and the city lay in Turkish hands. What followed was a full-scale slaughter of the Christian population, a massacre that Cypriot historians place at around 20,000 men, women and children. They

An early 17th-century Venetian model of a Turkish *Sultana* (flagship) galley. The *lanterna* of Ali Pasha would probably have been similar in appearance and oar arrangement to this model. (Civici Musei Veneziana d'arte e di storia, Venice)

The appointment of Don John of Austria to the command of the Fleet of the Holy League by Pope Pius V in early 1571. The appointment ensured the union of the Christian maritime powers in the Mediterranean. Bas relief from the Basilica Santa Maria Maggiore, Rome. (Stratford Archive)

Pope Pius V appointed the Spanish general Marc Antonio Colonna as the commander of his papal fleet in a move calculated to win the support of Philip II for his crusade against the Turks. Bas relief from the Basilica Santa Maria Maggiore, Rome. (Stratford Archive)

add that only about 1,000 inhabitants survived; children and young women, destined for the slave markets. Within weeks of the fall of Nicosia, Turkish troops had overrun the rest of the island, encountering little or no resistance apart from at Famagusta, where the port was still held by the Venetians. By 18 September Mustapha Pasha's army was encamped outside Famagusta, and envoys were sent in to discuss surrender terms with the city's Governor, Marc Antonio Bragadino. To encourage his prompt surrender, the envoys presented him with the severed head of Nicolo Dandolo. Unperturbed, Bragadino refused to surrender. Faced with a spirited defence, Mustapha Pasha ordered siege lines to be dug, and sited his siege guns where they could bombard the defences and cover the approaches to the harbour. Before the Turkish fleet arrived to complete the isolation of the city, Bragadino sent a squadron to Venice, requesting that a fleet be sent to relieve the city.

THE FORMATION OF THE HOLY LEAGUE

The Venetians clearly needed help, but they found themselves hindered by the policy of neutrality which they had followed for three decades. The new Doge of Venice, Alvise Moncenigo I had been part of a ruling council which had remained immune to the crusading rhetoric of the Pope and Philip II. Now he and his council found themselves in a position where they had to use the same crusading propaganda in an attempt to gain the support of the rest of Christian Europe. Moncenigo was well aware that Venice alone lacked the naval power to wrest Cyprus from the Turks. Besides, the Republic's naval commanders steadfastly refused to risk their entire galley fleet in an unsupported foray into the eastern Mediterranean. Put simply, without its galley fleet, Venice and her Mediterranean 'empire' were defenceless, and the loss of her fleet would be a calamity. Having refused to participate in the religious war against Islam, the Venetian ambassadors were understandably pessimistic about their chances of soliciting aid from Philip II and Pope Pius V. Consequently, envoys were sent to conduct secret negotiations with the Sultan at the same time as the Venetian ambassadors were preaching for a new crusade to recapture Cyprus from the Muslims. Like much of Mediterranean politics in the 16th century, religion proved less of an obstacle to diplomacy than economics and dynastic rivalry.

By early August 1571 little diplomatic headway had been made in Rome, Madrid or Constantinople. The Venetian galley fleet occupied itself with raids against Turkish ports in the Adriatic, then sailed to Crete, where it waited for further orders. Suddenly, everything changed. Pope Pius V was a pious man, and resented the loss of any Christian territory to the Turks. He agreed to back the Venetians, and wrote a personal appeal to Philip II, requesting the support of 'His Catholic Majesty' in the formation of a 'Holy League' of Christian powers to rescue Cyprus from the Muslim invaders. Philip was embroiled in the *Morisco* revolt, and was wary of any alliance with Venice. He agreed to aid the Pope and the Doge, but stopped short of joining any formal alliance. Instead he ordered his Sicilian galley squadron of 49 vessels commanded by the Genoese *condottiere* Andrea Doria to co-operate with the Venetians. Given the intense animosity between Venice and Genoa, the selection guaranteed disunity in

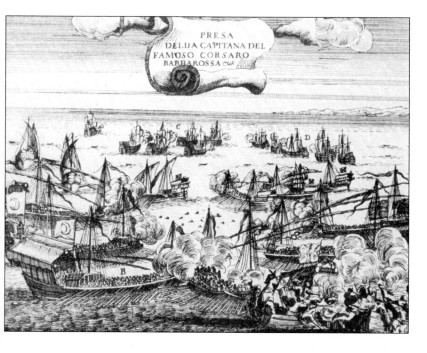

Entitled 'The capture of the flagship of the famous Corsair Barbarossa', the subject was more wistful than historical. The Barbary Corsair Khaireddin Barbarossa (1483–1546) was a master tactician, and rose to command the Turkish galley fleet during the victory at Prevesa in 1538. (Stratford Archive)

the Christian ranks. For his part, the Pope appointed Marc Antonio Colonna as commander of the Papal contingent. A Roman nobleman, the 35-year-old Colonna was an experienced military commander, fighting in the Spanish service. More importantly, he was also a skilled diplomat. Given the animosity between the Venetians and their crusading allies, this was to be of prime importance. He commanded a small contingent of 12 galleys.

The Venetian fleet at anchor in the Cretan port of Candia consisted of some 120 galleys, but most vessels lacked the crew and supplies necessary to undertake offensive action. While fresh crews were recruited, Girolamo

The battle of Djerba (May 1560) was a major disaster for the Christians, and led directly to the creation of a new and improved galley fleet by both the Spanish and the Venetians. Detail of 'The Massacre of Djerba', an oil painting by Tintoretto. (Museo del Prado, Madrid)

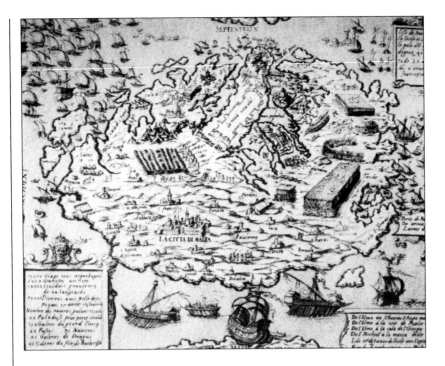

The Turkish siege of Malta in 1565 marked the most westward penetration of the Ottoman Turkish fleet into the western Mediterranean. The failure to capture the island was a severe blow to Turkish prestige, and led directly to the assault on Cyprus five years later as a means of revitalising the Turkish maritime campaign against Christendom. (Clyde Hensley Collection)

Zanne, the Venetian commander, elected to wait for the Spanish and Papal allies to arrive. Meanwhile, Nicosia was being besieged. On 1 September Andrea Doria and Marc Antonio Colonna sailed into Suda Bay, where Zanne was watering his fleet. Following a Council of War the decision was made to continue the offensive. By locating and destroying the Turkish fleet, the army of Mustapha Pasha would be isolated on Cyprus, forcing the Sultan to sue for peace. Two weeks later the combined fleet of 180 galleys sailed to the south-west corner of Asia Minor, via the Venetian-held island of Scarpanto. As the galleys lay off the Anatolian headland of Castel Rosso, word reached the fleet of the fall of Nicosia. Worse still, Piali Pasha was reportedly at Rhodes with 200 galleys, threatening the Christian fleet's line

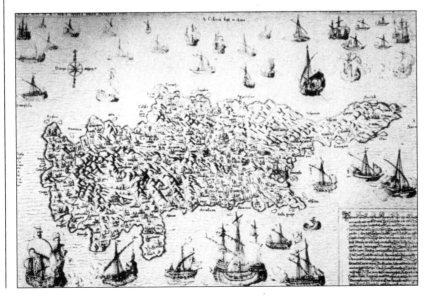

Cyprus at the time of the Turkish invasion of the Venetian-held island in 1570. The initial Turkish landings were made on the north coast, and the veteran Turkish troops managed to conquer the island in 70 days, although the port of Famagusta held out for a further eight months. (Clyde Hensley Collection)

of communications with its base at Candia. On 19 September another council of war was held. Andrea Doria refused to continue, claiming that his Spanish contingent was only available for combined operations until the end of the month, when it would have to return to Sicily. Zanne lost his nerve and ordered the entire fleet to return to Candia, claiming it was too late in the season to continue operations. Marc Antonio Bragadino in Famagusta would have to fend for himself until a fresh relief attempt could be made in the spring. Within weeks the fleet dissolved, the Venetian galleys returning to Corfu, and the Christian allies to Messina and Naples. A small Venetian squadron of 12 galleys remained in Candia to protect Crete.

For his part, Piali Pasha had indeed moved his fleet to Rhodes, leaving a small blockading squadron in place at Famagusta. When the Christian fleet withdrew, he dispersed the fleet, sending part to Constantinople and keeping the rest at Rhodes. His decision not to maintain a larger squadron off Famagusta would prove a costly mistake. The 12 Venetian galleys guarding Crete were commanded by the resourceful Antonio Quirini, who was determined to provide relief for Bragadino and his garrison. He loaded supplies onto four sailing ships, and embarked Candia's garrison of 1,600 Venetian soldiers on to his galleys. Quirini's force then sailed to Cyprus, arriving off Famagusta on 26 January 1571. He brushed aside the

Turkish blockading squadron, and landed his troops and supplies the
following morning.

Both Piali Pasha and Girolamo Zanne were removed from command
for their failures during the 1570 campaign. The aristocratic Sebastian
Venier was made the new Captain General of the Venetian fleet, while
Piali Pasha's second-in-command, Müezzenzade Ali Pasha, became the
new Kapudan Pasha (Fleet Commander) of the Turkish galley fleet. For
the rest of the winter both Christians and Turks prepared themselves for
a fresh campaign the following year.

During the winter of 1570/71, Venetian and Papal diplomats roamed
Europe, soliciting even greater support for their 'Holy League' against
the Turks. Despite their efforts, the diplomats produced little in the way
of material support. In Italy, Cosimo de Medici (the Duke of Tuscany)
supplied 12 galleys (which were attached to the Papal contingent), and
the Duke of Savoy provided three reinforcements for the Spanish fleet.

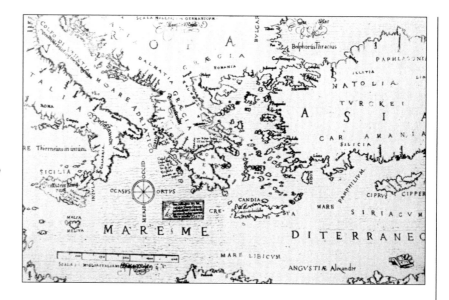

In this contemporary map of the central Mediterranean, the location of the battle of Lepanto is marked by two small Christian and Muslim banners. Compared with other examples of contemporary cartography, this map is extremely accurate, emphasising the importance of the region to the Venetian government, who hired the cartographers. (National Maritime Museum, Greenwich, London)

The Knights of Malta also provided a small force of three galleys, but these were all token contingents. What the allies needed was whole squadrons, not a handful of galleys. Any hope that the French might join the Holy League were dashed when the 20-year-old Charles IX (reigned 1560–74) refused to help, citing the military and financial attrition caused by the French Wars of Religion, which had just ended following the Peace of St Germaine-en-Laye (1570). The Emperor Maximilian also declared his hands were tied by the terms of his treaty with Selim II.

Help finally came from Philip II of Spain, who declared that his Spanish and Neapolitan squadrons would reinforce his Sicilian squadron. This meant that apart from a squadron retained to guard against attack by the Barbary Corsairs, the entire Spanish Mediterranean

This Venetian engraving shows the ideal deployment of a galley fleet, supported by sailing 'roundships' and by *galleasses*. Based on the action between the Christian left wing and the Turkish right at Lepanto, the diagram emphasises the use of a 'forlorn hope' of galleys or *galleasses* to break up the Turkish attack. (Biblioteca Nacional, Madrid)

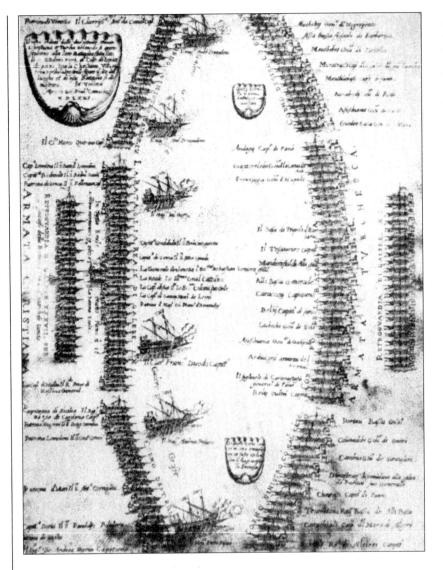

A simplified contemporary depiction of the battle, this engraving provides valuable clues concerning the position of the various commanders on both sides at the start of the battle. Although this appears useful, inaccuracies such as the presence of the two *galleasses* in advance of the Christian right wing cast doubt on the veracity of the information. (Biblioteca Nacionale, Barcelona)

galley fleet was committed to the campaign. Philip also appointed his 26-year-old half-brother Don John of Austria as commander of his fleet. Don John had only just finished quashing the *Morisco* revolt, and it would take him time to prepare his fleet for the coming campaign. A skilled diplomat, Don John's appointment by Philip II helped smooth over his earlier diplomatic gaffe of naming Andrea Doria as his fleet commander the previous year.

Pope Pius V was equally capable of making sound political decisions. Aware that the Venetians and the Turks were conducting secret peace negotiations, the Pontiff was eager to pre-empt any break-up of his informal Christian alliance. Consequently he ordered his cardinals to negotiate the formation of a formal alliance. The Venetians, the Spanish and even the smaller members of the potential alliance all had their own motives, and even objectives if the campaign continued into the following year. The Spanish wanted to crush Turkish naval power, thereby safeguarding Spanish territories in Italy from attack. The Venetians wanted a quick end to the war before her trading links were severed, but they also wanted to regain control of Cyprus. The Pope also wanted to wrest Cyprus from the Turks, but his principal motive was probably the establishment of Papal moral authority over the secular powers involved in the alliance. Both the Spanish and the Venetians demanded that their own commander be named as 'General at Sea' of the Holy League.

Finally, on 25 May 1571, the 'Holy League' was formed, and the alliance ratified by representatives of the Pope, the Doge, and of Philip II. Under its terms the League would undertake operations against the Turks and the course of the campaign be decided by the vote of three commanders. The Commander in Chief would put into practice the strategy decided by his three subordinates. Spain would assume responsibility for 50 per cent of the cost of the venture, Venice 35 per cent, the Papacy 15 per cent. A combined force of 200 galleys and 50,000 men would be available every spring, and the campaign would continue indefinitely. It was also agreed that Don John would act as Commander in Chief, supported by Marc Antonio Colonna, Sebastian Venier and Andrea Doria.

THE LEPANTO CAMPAIGN OF 1571

During the summer of 1571 the allied contingents straggled into Messina, and it was not until the end of August that the fleet of the Holy League was ready to begin offensive operations. By that time it was too late to save Famagusta.

By the start of May 1571 Antonio Bragadino and his 6,500 strong garrison had withstood the Turks for just over seven months. Two initial assaults had been launched the previous year, but unlike at Nicosia, the defenders were able to repulse the attacks. The Turks settled down to besiege the port, and during the winter 74 siege guns were emplaced around Famagusta, supported by almost 80,000 troops. Mustapha Pasha increased the pressure on the garrison on 1 May when his engineers announced the ground was suitable to attempt mining operations to undermine the walls. A week later his guns commenced a non-stop bombardment of the port, firing 5,000 balls on the first day alone. The walls were reduced to rubble, and Bragadino organised work parties to shore up the defences, while his troops repulsed Turkish attempts to break into the city. He even used walls of burning timber to deny breaches to the enemy, while the garrison worked behind the flames to improve the defences. After 12 days, the townspeople petitioned Bragadino to discuss surrender terms, and with no relief force expected, the Venetian commander had little option but to agree. He had virtually no powder left, his garrison had been reduced to just half strength, and after ten months of siege, he was running short of food.

Negotiations were opened with the Turks, and surrender terms were agreed on 4 August. Under the terms of the surrender, the garrison was to be repatriated to Crete, and the civilians spared. Mustapha Pasha had no intention of being so lenient. Once the garrison were embarked on the transports, the Venetian commanders visited the Turkish command tent to pay their respects. Mustapha Pasha had them killed, then attacked the unarmed Venetian troops on the waiting transports, slaughtering the entire garrison. Bragadino alone was spared, only to be tortured for several days before being flayed alive in the main square of Famagusta. Although

THE ADVANCE TO LEPANTO, MAY–OCTOBER 1571

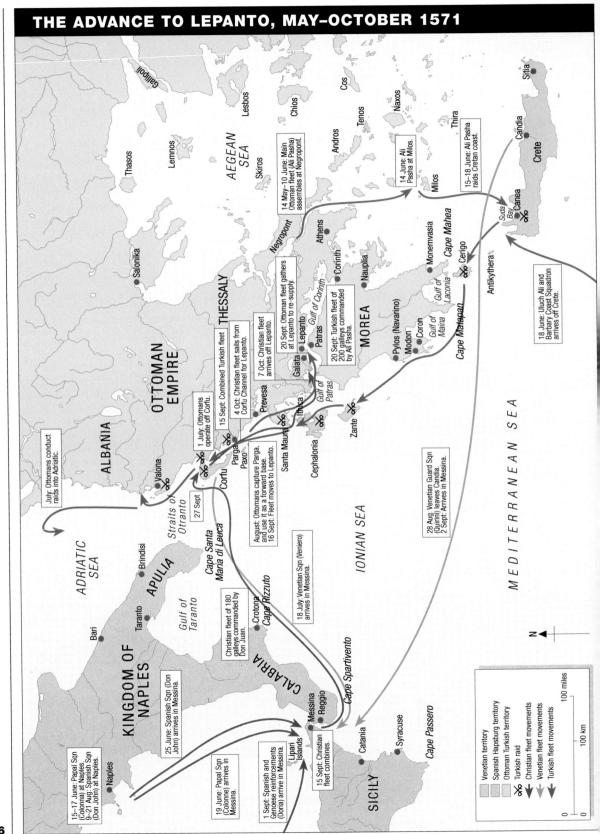

Map labels and annotations:

Gallipoli

AEGEAN SEA

Thasos

Lemnos

Lesbos

Chios

Cos

Skiros

Tenos

Andros

Naxos

Thira

Sitia

Candia

Crete

14 May–10 June: Main Ottoman fleet (Ali Pasha) assembles at Negropont.

14 June: Ali Pasha at Milos.

15–18 June: Ali Pasha raids Cretan coast.

Suda Bay

Canea

Salonika

Negropont

Athens

Corinth

Gulf of Corinth

Monemvasia

Cape Mahea

Cerigo

Antikythera

18 June: Uluch Ali and Barbary Coast Squadron arrives off Crete.

THESSALY

OTTOMAN EMPIRE

ALBANIA

July: Ottomans conduct raids into Adriatic.

Valona

15 Sept: Combined Turkish fleet

1 July: Ottomans operate off Corfu.

4 Oct: Christian fleet sails from Corfu Channel for Lepanto.

7 Oct: Christian fleet arrives off Lepanto.

20 Sept: Ottoman fleet gathers at Lepanto to re-supply.

Prevesa

Galata

Lepanto

Patras

Ithica

Gulf of Patras

MOREA

Nauplia

20 Sept: Turkish fleet of 200 galleys commanded by Ali Pasha.

Pylos (Navarino)

Coron

Modon

Gulf of Malia

Laconia

Cape Matapan

Parga

Paxo

Corfu

Santa Maura

August: Ottomans capture Parga, and use it as a forward base. 16 Sept: Fleet moves to Lepanto.

27 Sept

Cephalonia

Zante

Straits of Otranto

Cape Santa Maria di Leuca

ADRIATIC SEA

Brindisi

APULIA

Taranto

Bari

Gulf of Taranto

KINGDOM OF NAPLES

CALABRIA

Crotona
Cape Rizzuto

Christian fleet of 180 galleys commanded by Don Juan.

18 July: Venetian Sqn (Veniero) arrives in Messina.

IONIAN SEA

28 Aug: Venetian Guard Sqn (Quirini) leaves Candia. 2 Sept: Arrives in Messina.

MEDITERRANEAN SEA

Cape Spartivento

Messina

Reggio

Lipari Islands

15 Sept: Christian fleet combines.

Catania

Syracuse

Cape Passero

SICILY

25 June: Spanish Sqn (Don John) arrives in Messina.

19 June: Papal Sqn (Colonne) arrives in Messina.

1 Sept: Spanish and Genoese reinforcements (Doria) arrive in Messina.

15–17 June: Papal Sqn (Colonna) at Naples. 9–21 Aug: Spanish Sqn (Don John) at Naples.

Naples

N

100 miles
100 km

Legend:
- Venetian territory
- Spanish Hapsburg territory
- Ottoman Turkish territory
- Turkish raid
- Christian fleet movements
- Venetian fleet movements
- Turkish fleet movements

THE FLEETS CLOSE, 6–7 OCTOBER 1571

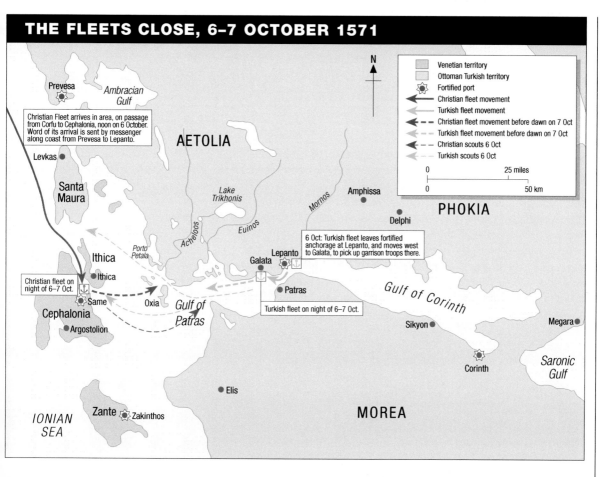

Prevesa

Ambracian Gulf

Christian Fleet arrives in area, on passage from Corfu to Cephalonia, noon on 6 October. Word of its arrival is sent by messenger along coast from Prevesa to Lepanto.

AETOLIA

Levkas

Santa Maura

Lake Trikhonis

Mornos

Amphissa

Delphi

PHOKIA

Legend:
- Venetian territory
- Ottoman Turkish territory
- Fortified port
- Christian fleet movement
- Turkish fleet movement
- Christian fleet movement before dawn on 7 Oct
- Turkish fleet movement before dawn on 7 Oct
- Christian scouts 6 Oct
- Turkish scouts 6 Oct

0   25 miles

0   50 km

Euinos

Acheloos

Porto Petala

Ithica

Ithica

Christian fleet on night of 6–7 Oct.

Same

Oxia

Cephalonia

Argostolion

Galata

Lepanto

6 Oct: Turkish fleet leaves fortified anchorage at Lepanto, and moves west to Galata, to pick up garrison troops there.

Patras

Gulf of Corinth

Gulf of Patras

Turkish fleet on night of 6–7 Oct.

Sikyon

Megara

Corinth

Saronic Gulf

Elis

MOREA

IONIAN SEA

Zante

Zakinthos

news of the Turkish betrayal incensed the Christians of Europe, the salutary lesson was understood perfectly by the Cypriots. Any attempt at resistance to Turkish authority would be brutally quashed. The Turks were then able to withdraw the bulk of their army, leaving a garrison of 22,000 men on the island.

News of the fall of Famagusta reached Messina in the first days of September. A Council of War was duly held to decide what to do next. Reports had reached Don John that the main Turkish fleet under Ali Pasha had gathered at Negropont in the Aegean, and had spent much of June raiding the northern coast of Crete. By the first week in July the Turks were off Corfu, and spent the next few weeks raiding Venetian ports on the Adriatic coast as far north as Ragusa. Turkish scouting vessels also probed westwards along the heel of Italy, looking for the Christian fleet which was expected to sail to relieve Famagusta. It was this Turkish fleet which would become the new focus for the Holy League. It was hoped that further incursions into the Adriatic could be discouraged by destroying Ali Pasha's fleet and capturing the Turkish bases in the Peloponnese, which served as stepping stones for a fleet sailing around Greece. Due to the constraints of water and supply storage, and the large number of men needed to operate a war galley, galley fleets were limited to short voyages of three to five days. This meant that fleets moved from base to base. By denying these 'stepping stones' to the enemy, control over areas of sea could be ensured.

The Christian fleet sailed from Messina on 16 September, and took four days to advance the 125 miles (200km) to Crotona, on the southern coast of Italy. Bad weather delayed the fleet for a week, but it crossed the Gulf of Taranto on 25 September, heading due east to reach Corfu two days later. The Venetian garrison brought the fleet commanders up to date with events. The Turks had raided the island, then headed south, and were reported to be using the port of Lepanto in the Gulf of Corinth as a new Adriatic base. Gil d'Andrada, the commander of the fleet's scouting squadron, also reported that the Turks were short of men due to sickness, and that their fleet consisted of around 200 galleys.

While the fleet anchored in Gomenizza Bay (on the Greek shore of the Corfu Channel), Don Juan inspected the fleet, condemning four Venetian galleys that were unfit for active service. He also tried to redistribute his available soldiers throughout the fleet, and in the process almost caused the collapse of the alliance. Most of the Venetian galleys were undermanned, and Spanish and Italian soldiers were used to augment the Venetian soldiers on board the galleys. Friction between the two groups caused a riot on one Venetian galley, so Sebastian Venier ordered the Spanish officer involved to be hung from the yardarm. This sparked a major incident, when Spanish and Venetian crews prepared to fight each other. Troops were armed, guns were loaded, and the two contingents squared off for a fight. Only the intervention of Marc Antonio Colonna prevented the fleet from tearing itself apart in an internecine fight. The following day, although Don John refused to deal with Venier in his councils of war, the fragile alliance was restored. Agostin Barbarigo became the new Venetian representative, and although tensions remained high, both sides were persuaded that the real enemy was the Turkish fleet, not each other.

On 3 October the fleet sailed south in search of the enemy. News of the treatment meted out to Marc Antonio Bragadino simply encouraged the Venetians to seek revenge against the Turks, helping to unite the Christian forces in common cause better than any pleading or rhetoric from the contingent commanders. Two days later the Christians were off Cephalonia, and Turkish scouts brought news of the Christian approach to Ali Pasha in Lepanto. The Turkish fleet prepared to sail west to meet their adversaries, while the Christians were encouraged by reports of Turkish preparations. Although neither side knew exactly how many ships and men were in their opponents' fleet, they both assumed they had an advantage, and both sides were eager for battle. The two greatest galley fleets ever assembled were about to clash. The forthcoming battle would be the last great crusading fight between Muslim and Christian, and the fate of the Mediterranean hung in the balance.

THE BATTLE OF LEPANTO

Like any naval battle before the advent of steam-powered warships, the battle began in an almost leisurely fashion, then turned into a frenetic clash of ships and men. When the leading ships of the Christian fleet passed through the gap between Scropha Point and Oxia into the Gulf of Patras, they caught their first glimpse of the Turkish fleet, some nine miles (14km) to the east. It was just before 7.30am. Given the speed of oar-powered ships, and the need to maintain formation, it would be at least two hours before the two fleets clashed; plenty of time for both sides to prepare themselves.

The Venetian admiral Barbarigo commanded the leading 'Battle' (division) of Christian galleys, and was the first senior Christian officer to see the enemy. He was unsure of the exact location of the shoals he knew fringed Scropha Point, so he elected to give his 'Battle' plenty of sea room. Consequently he waited until his flagship was approximately a mile past the point, then he turned his galley to port, giving the order to swing his division to port in succession as they passed him. As the rest of his 'Battle' passed the flagship, they turned to port, creating a mile-long line of galleys, stretching to the south-south-west, and facing eastwards towards the advancing Turks.

His 'Battle' now formed the left wing of the Christian fleet, and was slightly eastwards of the other 'battles', who passed astern of Barbarigo's galleys, heading south to take up their own battle positions. A few hundred yards south-west of the left 'Battle', the galleys of the central 'Battle', or 'main body' began to turn to port, slowly shaking themselves out into a line. Again, they turned in succession one after the other; an evolution that must have taken the best part of 30 minutes. The most southerly ship of this central 'Battle' was the *Capitana* of Malta. The rearguard, which now became the right wing 'Battle' followed on behind the centre, and Andrea Doria's galleys duly wheeled themselves into position to the south of the main 'Battle'. By 9.00am the entire Christian fleet had formed its battle line, with a few important exceptions. While the two *galleasses* attached to Barbarigo's command were able to take up positions in front of the Christian left wing, the other *galleasses* had further to travel. The fleet picked up speed as it passed Scropha Point, leaving the slower *galleasses* to follow on behind as best they could. As it would have taken the rear pair of *galleasses* (attached to Andrea Doria's 'Battle') a full 90 minutes to reach their position in front of Doria's galleys once they passed Scropha Point, they were still trying to catch up when the two lines clashed. Similarly the Christian reserve division commanded by Bazán was still moving south, towards its appointed position to the rear of the Christian centre. The two *galleasses* attached to the centre were also struggling to reach their assigned positions.

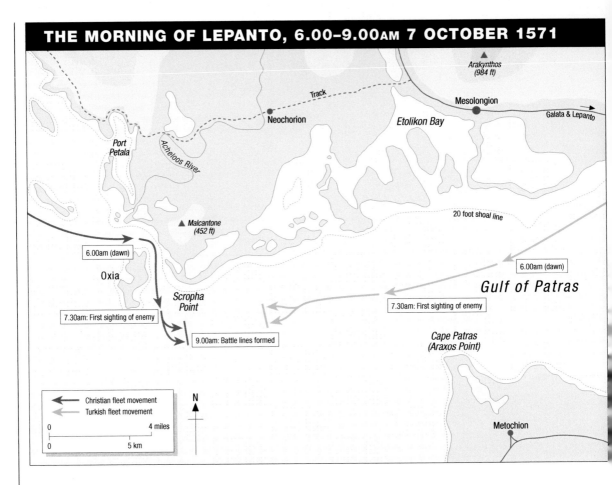

By 9.00am the Turkish fleet was already in position facing the Christians, and some four miles (6km) to the east. Its right wing was formed from its vanguard, commanded by Mehmet Sulik 'Scirocco', while Ali Pasha's main body became the Turkish centre. The left wing was formed from Uluch Ali's division. While the general orientation of the Turkish line was north to south, the three divisions were slightly echeloned. The right wing was slightly in advance of the centre, while the left wing was further behind Ali Pasha's galleys, almost in line with the Turkish reserve, which formed up behind the Turkish centre. It was also becoming apparent to the thousands of men who watched the fleets form their battle lines that the Turkish line overlapped the Christian line on both flanks. For his part, Barbarigo was unaffected by this, as he planned to keep well away from the shoals a mile to the north, off his left beam. Don John of Austria had already ordered a cannon to be fired, so that the Turkish commander could identify the Christian flagship. An answering shot came from Ali Pasha's flagship. This gentlemanly exchange identifying the two fleet flagships marked the civilised portion of the battle. Once the two fleets clashed, both sides would abandon all chivalric niceties in their fight with the 'infidel'.

The Turkish overlap did concern Andrea Doria, as his wing was unprotected by land and therefore his galleys could be outflanked and surrounded by those of Uluch Ali, in the Turkish division facing him. As for Uluch Ali himself, the Barbary Corsair was a superb naval tactician, and

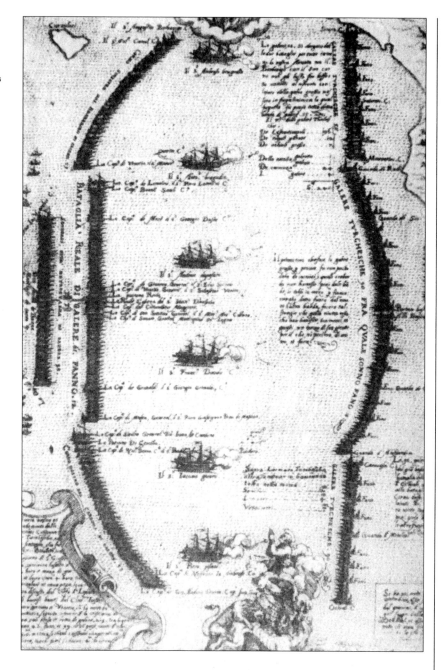

In this engraving, similar to that shown on p.44, the location of the northern shore of the Gulf of Patras has been added, albeit in the wrong place. Both engravings place Barbarigo on the extreme left of the Christian line, Andrea Doria on the extreme right, and both fleet commanders in the centre of their respective fleets. (Biblioteca Nacionale, Barcelona)

he was well aware of the opportunity the overlap presented to him. While the other Turkish and Christian division (or 'Battle') commanders were more inclined to close directly with the enemy, both Andrea Doria and Uluch Ali were more inclined to seek an advantage over their opponents before engaging. As the two were probably the finest sea officers on either side, this was hardly surprising. In addition, both the Barbary Corsairs and Andrea Doria's Genoese were mercenaries, and were probably unwilling to commit themselves to a brutal and destructive fight at close quarters unless the odds were favourable. While both commanders were criticised for their 'lack of aggressiveness' after the battle, both were simply using their skills to best effect. When Andrea Doria saw Uluch Ali's division edge even

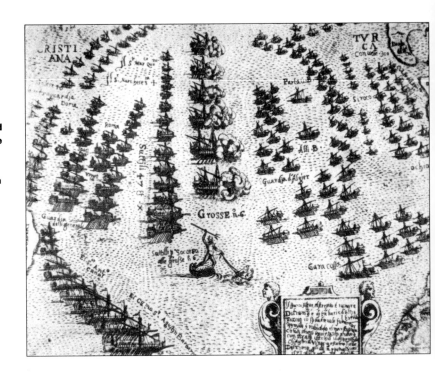

further south, he was forced to edge south himself, in order to prevent the Turks enveloping his wing. Naturally this led to an increasing gap between the right of the Christian centre and the most northerly galley of Andrea Doria's wing. Also, as the left and centre advanced slowly towards the east, the Christian right wing fell behind, as it was heading diagonally away from the rest of the fleet, towards the south-east. Inevitably, this prompted Uluch Ali to continue his move towards the south-west, as it maintained the threat to Doria's right flank. Ali was also aware that the sun would provide him with an advantage as the day wore on towards noon, as the Christians would be facing directly into its glare.

A Turkish galley approaching the Christian fleet. Interesting details include the deployment of short-bow archers in advance of the *arrumbada* (fighting platform), and the use of swivel guns to fire at targets off the port beam. Detail from a contemporary German engraving, dated 1575. (Author's Collection)

By 10.30am the northern and central divisions of both fleets were well within artillery range, and were closing with each other at a combined speed of around five knots. While far from the maximum possible speed available, the commanders of both sides wanted to maintain order, and the Christian battle plan demanded that the three pairs of *galleasses* precede the rest of the Christian line, although the *galleasses* attached to Andrea Doria's 'Battle' were still not in place, they were probably somewhere between the Christian centre and the reserve. Eight galleys that had scouted for the main fleet during the advance to the Gulf of Patras were seconded to Bazán's reserve division before the start of the battle. These were duly detailed off to help tow the last two *galleasses* into the gap opened between the Christian centre and the right wing.

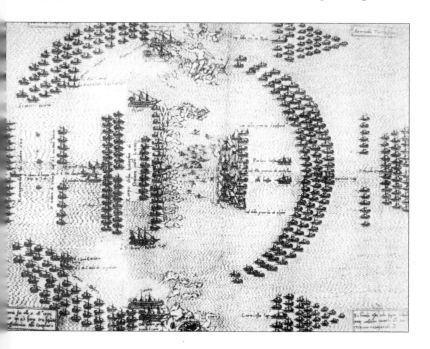

The approach of the two fleets. More an example of wishful thinking than accurate reconstruction, the two central *galleasses* are shown anchoring either end of the Christian centre, while the galleys between them are shown decimating the Turkish fleet with gunfire. In fact, the *galleasses* remained in front of the central galley line throughout the battle, and Christian gunnery was never as co-ordinated or effective as suggested here. (Museo Storico Navale, Madrid)

THE HOLY LEAGUE AND TURKISH BATTLE LINES CLOSE
(pages 54–55)

The Christian commander-in-chief Don John of Austria placed his *Real* (royal galley or fleet flagship) (1) in the centre of the line of the main Christian division. This was still an age when commanders fought in the front line, leading by example in the front rank of the central element of a battle-line. In this respect, Lepanto was similar to land battles of the late medieval and Renaissance periods. Don John was flanked by other senior Christian officers in their *lanternas* (2), creating a powerful block of warships that would both strengthen the centre and protect the commander. One of the few chivalric elements of the battle was the exchange of shots by Don John's *Real* and Ali Pasha's *Sultana* (3). This allowed the two commanders to identify their counterpart's flagship amid the mass of ships in the opposing battle line. Ali Pasha, who had been heading towards the Venetian *lanterna* of Sebastian Venier, promptly altered course and his flagship steered straight towards the *Real*. This scene shows the two battle lines shortly after the exchange of recognition shots. Don John is shown in the stern of his flagship, standing beneath his personal standard, which had been presented and blessed by the Pope (4). His vessel had 35 banks of oars each side, with a team of six men at each oar rowing in the 'alla scaloccio' manner. A large, cumbersome vessel, it set the pace for the fleet and consequently the battle lines inched towards each other at what must have seemed like an agonisingly slow pace. Both fleets advanced in line abreast (*en haye*) to maximise the effect of their artillery, with the galleys arrayed so their oars almost touched. Here we see only a section of the mile-long line of some 60 galleys. Similarly large formations were deployed on either flank and a small reserve was deployed behind the central division. Its task was to support the main fleet by moving troops up to reinforce threatened sections of the line. Just before the two fleets clashed, Don John ordered two galleys from the reserve to lie off his port and starboard quarter, ready to support the flagship if the need arose. In front of the flagship can be seen one of the two *galleasses* of the central division. These were posted in front of the Christian centre to disrupt the Turkish advance as it approached the Christian line (5). The *Real* carried a bow battery of five guns (6) – a *Cañon* (cannon), two *Media Culebrinas* (demi-culverins) and two *sacres* (sakers). This was typical of the powerful suite of ordnance carried in the larger Christian galleys and outgunned substantially the batteries fitted in the bows of their Turkish counterparts. The battery was supported by a selection of smaller *versos* (swivel guns) mounted on the fighting platform above the guns.
(Tony Bryan)

As the commander of the reserves, the task of Don Álvaro de Bazán was to watch developments, and to feed reinforcements into the three main 'Battles' at the points where they would have the greatest effect. This meant that although he had 38 galleys under his command (30 plus the advance force of eight galleys), this reserve was viewed more as a pool of manpower rather than as a manoeuvrable naval force in its own right. The Turks employed their reserve in the same manner, but had the advantage of a large number of small craft, allowing them to insert reinforcements with a little more rapidity that Bazán could with his larger galleys. Bazán duly rounded up all the ships' boats (known as *fragatine*) that he could find, and held them ready to transfer troops from ship to ship.

The two sides prepared for the inevitable clash. As both the Christian left wing 'Battle' and the Turkish right wing division were slightly ahead of the central and southern portions of the rival battle lines, it was clear that the first clash would take place in the north, between the galleys of Barbarigo and those of 'Sirocco'. At this point, shortly before the two sides clashed, observers on both sides noted the incredible spectacle. Between 150 and 200 galleys per side were formed into an approximate line abreast, and were closing with each other, the sun in the south-east reflecting off the armour of the waiting soldiers and deck fittings. In addition, every galley was richly decorated with banners, tapestries and pennons, creating a glittering, romantic impression to almost all of the observers. Soon this image of menacing beauty would be replaced by visions of incredible carnage as the two fleets clashed.

THE NORTHERN CLASH

As the battle was fought in three separate areas corresponding to the three wings of each fleet, I have elected to follow the developments in each area, rather than trying to produce a strictly chronological account of the entire battle.

By 10.00am, when the two northern wings began their approach towards each other, a light westerly wind had sprung up, which slightly slowed the advance of the Muslim galleys. The battle began around 10.20am, when one of the two *galleasses* attached to the central 'Battle' opened fire on the advancing Turks. As the range would have been over a mile (1.5km), the shot was more a demonstration than a serious attempt to inflict damage. The two *galleasses* of the northern 'Battle' were within range of the enemy, and they both opened fire around 10.30am. The two vessels were commanded by a pair of brothers: Ambrogio and Antonio Bragadino, whose kinsman Marc Antonio had been tortured and killed by the Turks at Famagusta. For them it was a matter of family revenge. They concentrated the fire of their long bow guns on one of the larger Turkish galleys, and hit their target with their third shot. The Turkish vessel was struck in the bow, just below her waterline, and she started to sink. According to Christian accounts (based on the interrogation of prisoners), Ali Pasha in the centre was supposed to have tugged at his beard in frustration, taking this early loss as a bad omen. Witnesses also claim that the beat of the Turkish drums, which called the stroke of the fleet's rowers, stopped for a few moments. Whatever the immediate effect of the loss was to the Turks, there was little time for contemplation, as within a few

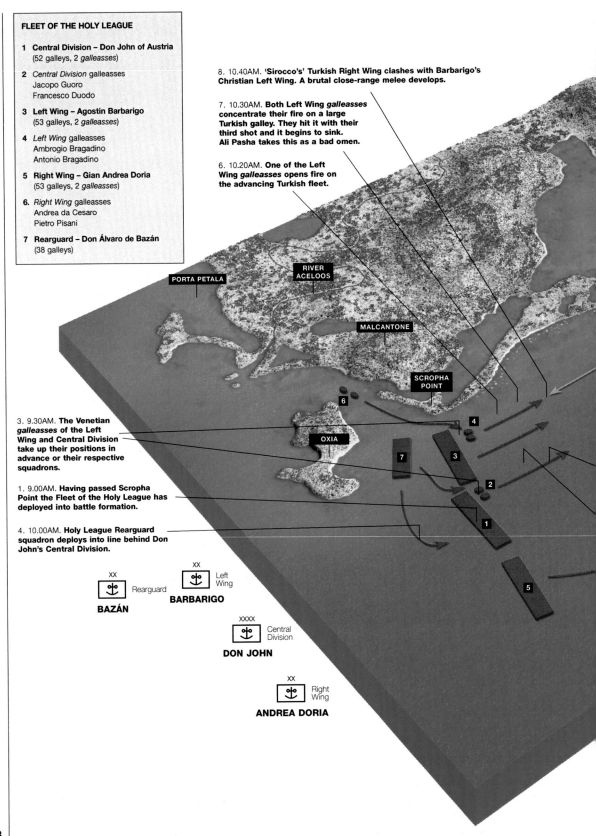

FLEET OF THE HOLY LEAGUE

1 **Central Division – Don John of Austria**
(52 galleys, 2 *galleasses*)

2 *Central Division* galleasses
Jacopo Guoro
Francesco Duodo

3 **Left Wing – Agostin Barbarigo**
(53 galleys, 2 *galleasses*)

4 *Left Wing* galleasses
Ambrogio Bragadino
Antonio Bragadino

5 **Right Wing – Gian Andrea Doria**
(53 galleys, 2 *galleasses*)

6. *Right Wing* galleasses
Andrea da Cesaro
Pietro Pisani

7 **Rearguard – Don Álvaro de Bazán**
(38 galleys)

8. 10.40AM. **'Sirocco's' Turkish Right Wing clashes with Barbarigo's Christian Left Wing. A brutal close-range melee develops.**

7. 10.30AM. **Both Left Wing *galleasses* concentrate their fire on a large Turkish galley. They hit it with their third shot and it begins to sink. Ali Pasha takes this as a bad omen.**

6. 10.20AM. **One of the Left Wing *galleasses* opens fire on the advancing Turkish fleet.**

PORTA PETALA

RIVER ACELOOS

MALCANTONE

SCROPHA POINT

OXIA

3. 9.30AM. **The Venetian *galleasses* of the Left Wing and Central Division take up their positions in advance or their respective squadrons.**

1. 9.00AM. **Having passed Scropha Point the Fleet of the Holy League has deployed into battle formation.**

4. 10.00AM. **Holy League Rearguard squadron deploys into line behind Don John's Central Division.**

XX
Rearguard
BAZÁN

XX
Left Wing
BARBARIGO

XXXX
Central Division
DON JOHN

XX
Right Wing
ANDREA DORIA

58

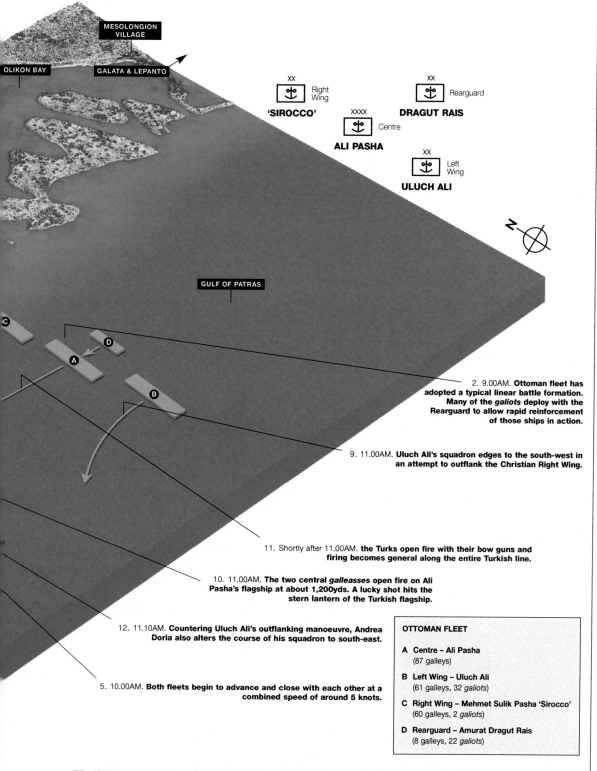

MESOLONGION VILLAGE

OLIKON BAY

GALATA & LEPANTO

XX
⚓ Right Wing

'SIROCCO'

XXXX
⚓ Centre

ALI PASHA

XX
⚓ Rearguard

DRAGUT RAIS

XX
⚓ Left Wing

ULUCH ALI

N

GULF OF PATRAS

C

D

A

B

2. 9.00AM. **Ottoman fleet has adopted a typical linear battle formation. Many of the** *galiots* **deploy with the Rearguard to allow rapid reinforcement of those ships in action.**

9. 11.00AM. **Uluch Ali's squadron edges to the south-west in an attempt to outflank the Christian Right Wing.**

11. Shortly after 11.00AM. **the Turks open fire with their bow guns and firing becomes general along the entire Turkish line.**

10. 11.00AM. **The two central** *galleasses* **open fire on Ali Pasha's flagship at about 1,200yds. A lucky shot hits the stern lantern of the Turkish flagship.**

12. 11.10AM. **Countering Uluch Ali's outflanking manoeuvre, Andrea Doria also alters the course of his squadron to south-east.**

5. 10.00AM. **Both fleets begin to advance and close with each other at a combined speed of around 5 knots.**

OTTOMAN FLEET

A Centre – Ali Pasha
(87 galleys)

B Left Wing – Uluch Ali
(61 galleys, 32 *galiots*)

C Right Wing – Mehmet Sulik Pasha 'Sirocco'
(60 galleys, 2 *galiots*)

D Rearguard – Amurat Dragut Rais
(8 galleys, 22 *galiots*)

BATTLE OF LEPANTO – THE FIRST CLASH

7 October 1571, 9.00am–11.10am, viewed from the south-west, showing the final advance to contact of the Holy League and Ottoman fleets as the Venetian *galleasses* struggle to take up their appointed positions. Weather is clear, wind 4–5 knots from west-north-west, tidal movement and currents are negligible.

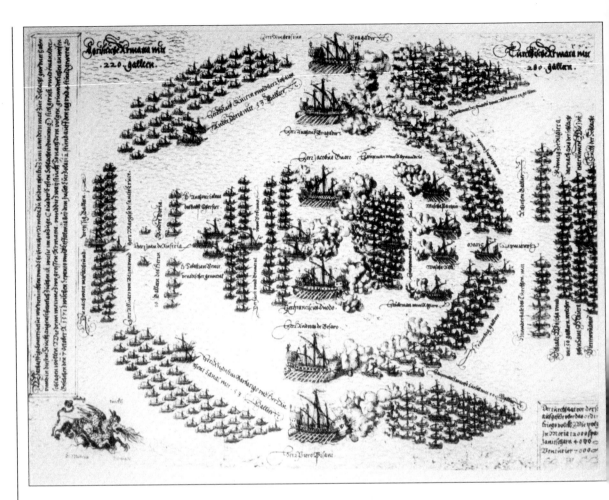

In this fanciful German engraving, the *galleasses* are shown in the correct place (apart from the two attached to the southern Christian 'Battle'), but all other aspects are incorrect, including the presence of a line of Turkish *lanternas* supporting the assault on the Christian centre. (National Maritime Museum, Greenwich, London)

minutes the leading Turkish galleys in the northern wing were approaching the two *galleasses*. The wing consisted of around 60 galleys, which split into three groups to pass the two ships, turning slightly to starboard as they did so. 'Sirocco', the Turkish wing commander, had local pilots on his staff, and he knew exactly where the shoals were to his north. He intended to pin the Christians in front of him using about two-thirds of his force, while the remaining and most northern group tried to work their way between the Christians and the shore. As an attempt at outflanking the Christians it was a half-hearted manoeuvre, as the Turks lacked sea room, but presumably 'Sirocco' planned to achieve a local superiority on one flank, then roll the Venetian line up from the north. Barbarigo noticed the change of direction and ordered his galleys to steer slightly to port, to try to close the gap on his left flank.

The two *galleasses* caused considerable damage to the closest Turkish galleys as the Muslim fleet rowed past them, heading for the main Christian line some 500 yards to the west. Although it is unlikely that more than one or two Turkish galleys were crippled in the exchange, the fire did disrupt the Turkish line, as galleys turned to avoid the *galleasses*, or were spun out of line as their oars were shot away by point blank fire. The northernmost *galleass* waddled round through 180 degrees to port backing water on her port side, and advancing on her starboard. Her guns were pointed at the vulnerable sterns of the Turkish squadron, and she

commenced a devastatingly accurate fire. The more southerly of the two Venetian *galleasses* (commanded by Antonio Bragadino) stayed in place, firing on the Turkish galleys of the central 'Battle' off her starboard side, and fighting off attempts to board her by the smaller Turkish vessels of the northern wing. At about 10.40am, the two northern wings clashed, the galleys firing off their ordnance immediately before the two sides clashed. Like two charging knights, the clash of wood, steel and flesh could be heard as far off as the southern wings, some three miles (5km) away.

The melee was a desperate affair, as neither side had much room to manoeuvre. Even worse for the Christians, 'Sirocco' had won his race, albeit with only a part of his force. Seven Turkish galleys managed to slip past the Christian left flank, a position held by Barbarigo in his flagship. The wing commander ordered his galley and those closest to him to turn to face the threat, but only part of the Christian left wing managed to react in time. When the two sides clashed, four Venetian galleys were caught in the flank and sunk before the galleys around Barbarigo could turn to port to meet the Turkish outflanking force head on. Only the disorder in the Turkish line caused by the fire from the *galleasses* prevented the outflanking element and the main Turkish force on the northern wing from smashing the Christian line. This Christian commander was situated at the point of greatest danger, and at one point, five Turkish galleys surrounded Barbarigo's *lanterna*, whose crew fought to repel boarding attempts from all directions. Around 11.15am Barbarigo's young nephew, Marino Contarini, moved up from the reserve squadron to support his uncle in his *Santa Magdalena* of Venice, but was struck down in the melee surrounding the *lanterna*. The fight continued, and as one observer put it, 'the sky could not be seen for arrows and shot. It was noon and yet it was dark from the smoke of the trombe and the pignatte [ordnance and grenades], and of

The battle on the northern wing centred around an attempt by the Turks to infiltrate between the Christian left flank and the shore to the north. Although partially successful, the majority of the attackers became embroiled in a melee around the flagship of Agostin Barbarigo, and the outflanking attempt failed. Detail from 'The Battle of Lepanto', a painting by the Italian School, late 16th century. (National Maritime Museum, Greenwich, London)

many fire projectiles which were inextinguishable even in the water.' While the Christians were hard-pressed, help was at hand.

The outflanking attempt by 'Sirocco' had been partially successful, but it also presented the Christians with an opportunity to isolate the Turkish right wing force. Marco Quirini, the *Proveditor* (Fleet Quartermaster) of Venice, commanded the right flank of the Christian left wing. He noted that while the melee was fierce around the opposite (northern) end of the line, the Christian ships in the southern portion of the wing remained unengaged, as the Turks gathered around Barbarigo and his consorts. The new course taken by the Turkish ships to the north had left Quirini free to manoeuvre, and this is exactly what he decided to do. On his own initiative he ordered the unengaged portion of the Christian left wing to wheel round to the north, a movement an observer likened to a door swinging on its hinges. He caught the Turks in the flank, and then in their rear pinning them against the reef, and against Barbarigo's galleys. The fight increased in its intensity as the Turks realised they were trapped between a reinforced enemy and a line of deadly shoals.

At first Barbarigo took little part in the fighting around him, as his age prevented him from joining his crew in the melee. Instead, he took up a position beneath the mainmast of his flagship, directing the action as best he could. It must have been a confusing scene, as visibility was down to a few yards, and the galleys of both sides had become somewhat intermingled. Shortly before noon, Barbarigo tried to give an order which his subordinates were unable to understand for the noise. He raised the visor of his helmet to speak more clearly, and at that moment a Turkish arrow struck him in the right eye, and he fell to the deck at the

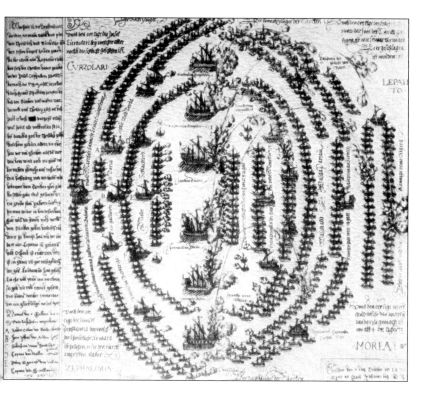

feet of his Flag Captain, Federico Nani. The wound was a mortal one, and he was carried beneath the *corsia* to safety. Although Venetian resistance on the flagship faltered for a few moments, Nani returned to rally his men, and the Turks were kept at bay until reinforcements were summoned. A galley from the reserves came to the rescue, and its crew forced the Turks off the flagship.

The tide of battle was now turning. Realising that their avenue of escape was cut off, many of the Turks gave up the fight, and ran for the relative safety of the shoals. Others continued the fight, but increasingly they were outnumbered as fresh Christian ships arrived, or were released when their Turkish opponents fled, allowing the Christian galleys to enjoy an increasing local superiority in numbers. In some of the Turkish galleys, Christian galley slaves had been able to free themselves, and had revolted against their masters, causing confusion and disorder in the Turkish fleet. On 'Sirocco's' flagship, the slaves succeeded in driving the now badly wounded Turkish commander and his men from the ship. Fortunately some galleys beached or grounded in the shoal water, while small *fustas* ferried survivors to the friendly shore. The envelopment initiated by Marco Quirini had proved decisive, as the Turks were left with little room to manoeuvre. Increasingly, they were driven back onto the shoals, while other vessels simply fled the fight, running themselves aground in order to save the crew – it was a well-established tenet of galley warfare that the crew and the guns were more important than the ship itself. Many of the small *fustas* formed a 'bridge' to the beach, allowing the Turks to scramble from galley to galley until they reached the safety of the marshy shore beyond. The high ground of the Malcantone, a small hill rising from the marsh, became a rallying point for the Turkish survivors, and as the Turkish opposition collapsed, several Venetian galleys spun round to fire their guns

Ali Pasha, the Turkish commander is shown directing the course of the battle from the stern of his *Sultana*, on the left of the picture. In fact, Ali Pasha grabbed a bow and fought with his archers once the two fleets clashed. Oil painting by Andrea Vicentino. (Palazzo Ducale, Venice)

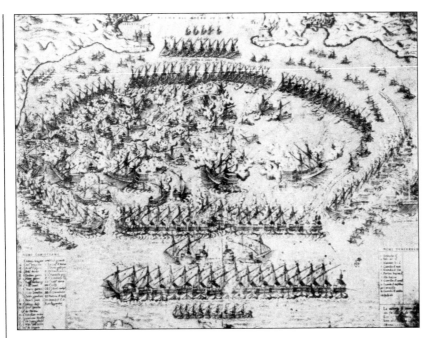

LEFT In this confused Italian depiction an attempt has been made to label the leading Christian galleys. Otherwise its only accurate feature remains the depiction of the battle starting on the northern flank before the southern flank was engaged, and in the presence of reserve squadrons behind the centre of both fleets. (Bibliotec Nacionale, Madrid)

at the Turks clustered around the hill. The battle petered out by 1.00pm, as the last of the Turkish crews gave up the fight or were overpowered. An entire Turkish wing had been destroyed, and Barbarigo's last fight proved to be a victorious one.

Christian landing parties clambered along the line of Turkish galleys to the shore, driving the remaining Turks inland, away from the fight. Hundreds of wounded Turks were captured, including 'Sirocco', who was duly taken as a prisoner back to the flagship of Marco Quirini. Severely wounded, he asked to be killed as a humanitarian gesture, and the following day he was duly shot by his captors, soon after Barbarigo had finally died from his eye wound, while 'thanking God for his victory'. While Barbarigo had certainly held the Turkish attack, the real hero of the northern fight was Quirini, whose initiative had turned an indecisive melee into a decisive victory.

THE BATTLE IN THE CENTRE

When Don John and Ali Pasha exchanged 'recognition shots' shortly before the two northern wings clashed (they probably fired just after 10.30am), the two fleet commanders demonstrated their willingness to fight 'in the old manner', a chivalric notion of tournaments and personal challenges that was fast becoming irrelevant in naval warfare. Both commanders knew where their opponent's flagship was, and they both duly steered towards each other.

At 11.00am or just afterwards, the two *galleasses* in front of the Christian line opened fire on Ali Pasha's flagship at a range of about 1,200 yards (1,000m). One of these shots struck the stern lantern of the Turkish flagship, a lucky shot given the range. Naturally, the Turkish commander saw this as another bad omen.

The *galleasses* had also demonstrated their potency, and the advancing Turkish centre veered away from them, forming three groups to pass them by. As was the case with the northern wing, the tendency was for the galleys closest to the *galleasses* to shy away from them, which led to crowding, and the disruption of the attacking line. Galleys collided, spars and oars were lost, and there was a strong possibility of the attack faltering. Ali ordered his galleys to slow down, countering the natural tendency to race past the *galleasses* as quickly as possible. Although it increased the exposure of his ships to the *galleasses'* broadsides, it reduced the disorder caused by bunching.

Shortly after 11.00am the Turks opened fire with their bow guns and firing became general all along the Turkish line. By contrast, the Christians preferred to follow the Spanish tactic of reserving their fire until the last possible moment before the two lines clashed. Like the Turks, the Christian advance was a slow, methodical one, with the emphasis on good order and the maintenance of formation rather than a headlong advance. At 11.35am, some five minutes before the two lines clashed, Ali Pasha's *Capitana* (or *Sultana*, to use the correct Turkish term) altered course slightly to starboard, as the bunching of the central group of galleys had forced it away from Don John's flagship. Christian observers claim that the middle of the three groups of the Turkish central 'Battle' was heading directly towards the *Capitana* of Venice (commanded by Sebastian Venier).

OPPOSITE **A more accurate depiction of Ali Pasha, standing on a platform behind the broken mainmast of his galley, armed with a short bow. Other Turkish archers and small-arms men line the *corsia* (central walkway) and the *arrumbada* (bow fighting platform). Note the large stern lantern, a symbol of command. Detail from 'The Battle of Lepanto', a painting by the Italian School, late 16th century. (National Maritime Museum, Greenwich, London)**

65

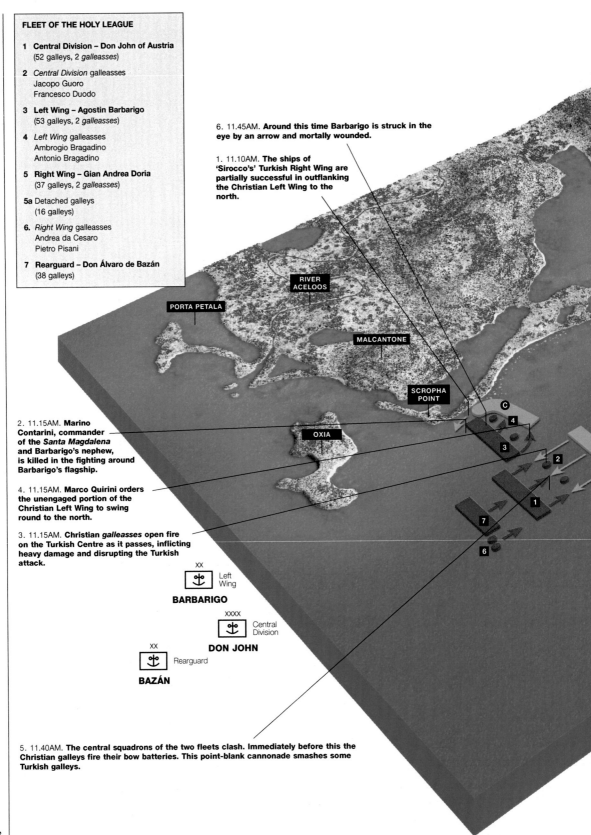

FLEET OF THE HOLY LEAGUE

1. **Central Division – Don John of Austria**
   (52 galleys, 2 *galleasses*)

2. *Central Division* galleasses
   Jacopo Guoro
   Francesco Duodo

3. **Left Wing – Agostin Barbarigo**
   (53 galleys, 2 *galleasses*)

4. *Left Wing* galleasses
   Ambrogio Bragadino
   Antonio Bragadino

5. **Right Wing – Gian Andrea Doria**
   (37 galleys, 2 *galleasses*)

5a. Detached galleys
   (16 galleys)

6. *Right Wing* galleasses
   Andrea da Cesaro
   Pietro Pisani

7. **Rearguard – Don Álvaro de Bazán**
   (38 galleys)

6. 11.45AM. **Around this time Barbarigo is struck in the eye by an arrow and mortally wounded.**

1. 11.10AM. **The ships of 'Sirocco's' Turkish Right Wing are partially successful in outflanking the Christian Left Wing to the north.**

RIVER ACELOOS

PORTA PETALA

MALCANTONE

SCROPHA POINT

OXIA

2. 11.15AM. **Marino Contarini, commander of the *Santa Magdalena* and Barbarigo's nephew, is killed in the fighting around Barbarigo's flagship.**

4. 11.15AM. **Marco Quirini orders the unengaged portion of the Christian Left Wing to swing round to the north.**

3. 11.15AM. **Christian *galleasses* open fire on the Turkish Centre as it passes, inflicting heavy damage and disrupting the Turkish attack.**

XX
Left Wing
BARBARIGO

XXXX
Central Division
DON JOHN

XX
Rearguard
BAZÁN

5. 11.40AM. **The central squadrons of the two fleets clash. Immediately before this the Christian galleys fire their bow batteries. This point-blank cannonade smashes some Turkish galleys.**

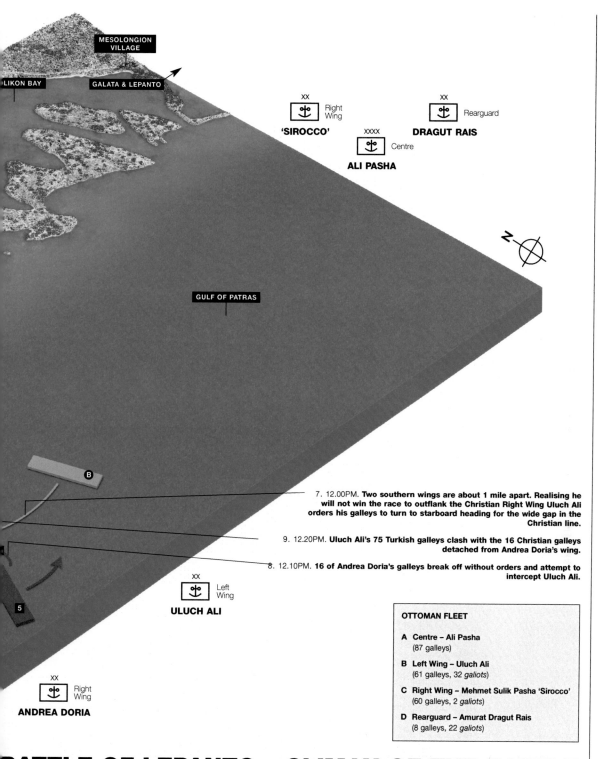

MESOLONGION VILLAGE

LIKON BAY

GALATA & LEPANTO

XX
⚓ Right Wing

'SIROCCO'

XXXX
⚓ Centre

ALI PASHA

XX
⚓ Rearguard

DRAGUT RAIS

N

GULF OF PATRAS

B

7. 12.00PM. **Two southern wings are about 1 mile apart. Realising he will not win the race to outflank the Christian Right Wing Uluch Ali orders his galleys to turn to starboard heading for the wide gap in the Christian line.**

9. 12.20PM. **Uluch Ali's 75 Turkish galleys clash with the 16 Christian galleys detached from Andrea Doria's wing.**

8. 12.10PM. **16 of Andrea Doria's galleys break off without orders and attempt to intercept Uluch Ali.**

XX
⚓ Left Wing

ULUCH ALI

5

XX
⚓ Right Wing

ANDREA DORIA

OTTOMAN FLEET

A **Centre – Ali Pasha**
(87 galleys)

B **Left Wing – Uluch Ali**
(61 galleys, 32 *galiots*)

C **Right Wing – Mehmet Sulik Pasha 'Sirocco'**
(60 galleys, 2 *galiots*)

D **Rearguard – Amurat Dragut Rais**
(8 galleys, 22 *galiots*)

BATTLE OF LEPANTO – CLIMAX OF THE BATTLE

7 October 1571, 11.10–12.20pm, viewed from the south-west, showing the struggle at its height as 'Sirocco' attempts to outflank the Christian fleet to the north, the fleets' central divisions clash in a bitter melee and Uluch Ali and Andrea Doria manoeuvre to the south. Weather is clear, wind 4–5 knots from west-north-west, tidal movement and currents are negligible

A cluster of Christian galleys fighting in line abreast, a formation considered ideal in galley warfare. In the foreground, Christian soldiers with boarding pikes and sword and buckler wait for a chance to board an enemy vessel. Detail from 'The Battle of Lepanto'. (National Maritime Museum, Greenwich, London).

Ali Pasha had no intention of attacking anyone other than the fleet commander, so his change of course aimed the central group of galleys directly towards Don John's *Real*.

Don John, Sebastian Venier and Marco Antonio Colonna were stationed at different points in the Christian centre, but each was supported by additional galleys. These were ordered to take station behind them, so they could throw in reserves to protect the flagships. They knew that the fighting would be fiercest around the three flagships as the Turks would target these prestigious vessels in particular. For his part, Ali Pasha was flanked by Pertau Pasha and another two escorting galleys, while six more galleys were ordered to remain to the rear of the fleet flagship, to offer support when needed.

At 11.40am the two lines clashed, preceded by a rolling discharge of the bow ordnance of all the galleys in the Christian centre. This point blank fire halted several Turkish galleys, their superstructures crushed but the rest came on with an extra spurt of speed. The two fleet flagships crashed into each other, and both Spanish arquebusiers and Turkish bowmen and musket men fired onto the crowded decks of their opponent. Grenades and incendiary bombs were hurled all along the line, grappling irons snaked between the ships, and as oars splintered and hulls clashed together, the swordsmen of both sides took the fight to the enemy. This was no subtle battle involving manoeuvre, but a grinding, head-on clash between two powerful galley fleets. Ali Pasha himself picked up his composite bow and joined his archers in the bow of his flagship. He had no more orders to give, and as his skill with a bow

The deck of Don John's *Real* during the climax of the battle in the centre. Spanish arquebusiers are shown firing at men in the water, while other Christian galleys move up in support. Detail from a contemporary German engraving, dated 1575. (Author's Collection)

was legendary, he could do more damage shooting than simply waiting for either victory or defeat. He was probably the last commander of a European or Mediterranean army or navy to use a bow in combat.

The melee centred around the two flagships sucked in several additional galleys, as the reserves of both sides fed fresh troops into the fight. Soldiers with swords, bucklers, half-pikes and even axes were more useful in this kind of fight than troops equipped with firearms, as targets were difficult to distinguish in the press of men and ships, the smoke from the grenades and ordnance, and the general confusion of a disorientating melee. Venier in his *Capitana* of Venice forced his way through the Turkish centre to reach the stern of Ali Pasha's flagship. Like other senior commanders, Venier left the hand-to-hand fighting to younger men. Taking up a crossbow he stationed himself amidships in his *Capitana* and joined the fight. On the starboard side of the *Real*, Marco Antonio Colonna in the Papal *Capitana* also managed to thread his way through the fighting to reach Pertau Pasha's flagship. Don John's and Ali Pasha's flagships were fast becoming a magnet for the galleys of the centre of both sides. By noon some 30 Christian and Turkish galleys were crammed into an incredibly small space, measuring no more than 250 yards from north to south, and less than 200 yards east to west. This mass of ships became the real killing ground of the battle. Although the other two groups of galleys in the Turkish 'centre' (one to the north, the other to the south) tried to re-form some sort of line and pushed forward into the Christian fleet, the heaviest of the fighting was in the very centre.

Ali Pasha's men boarded Don John's *Real* across the forecastle and captured its *arrumbada* (the fighting platform built over the bow artillery), but were unable to push forward any further. Sebastian Venier ranged alongside the flagship, reinforcing Don John at this crucial stage of the fighting, just as more Turkish reinforcements were arriving behind Ali Pasha's flagship. At the same time, Don Álvaro de Bazán was feeding in some of his reserves. One of these, the *Faith* of Venice (commanded by Giovanni Battista Contarini) rammed and sunk one of

The stern of a Spanish *lanterna* is shown lined with arquebusiers, while other crewmen spear Turkish survivors in the water with boarding pikes. In the battle, little quarter was given or expected by either side. Detail from a contemporary German engraving, dated 1575. (Author's Collection)

THE VENETIAN *GALLEASSES* BREAK UP THE TURKISH BATTLE LINE (pages 70–71)

The Christian fleet at Lepanto was divided into three main divisions (or 'battles') and a reserve. Don John of Austria's plan was for the six Venetian *galleasses* that accompanied the fleet to take up position slightly ahead of the main Christian line, with two *galleasses* attached to each of the main divisions. While the two *galleasses* seconded to the Vanguard (northern wing) had little difficulty deploying in front of their division, the two attached to the Central Division were hard pushed to reach their designated positions ahead of the Christian fleet before the battle began. The remaining pair of *galleasses* attached to Andrea Doria's Rearguard (southern wing) never managed to take up position, and instead were thrust into battle alongside those elements of the reserve sent to assist Andrea Doria during the battle. This failure resulted from inability of the *galleasses* to manoeuvre with the same speed and dexterity as the galleys in the fleet. Converted from the hulls of large, broad-beamed 'merchant galleys', the Venetian *galleasses* (1) were slow and cumbersome under oars, with an extremely poor turning arc and performed little better under sail. Neither fish nor fowl, their one great attribute was their armament. A round forecastle was fitted in place of the gun platform of a normal galley (2). Well protected from enemy fire, this structure acted like a mini fortress capable of engaging targets to its front and to both port and starboard. In addition the *galleasses* carried smaller guns along the length of their rowing platforms, providing additional firepower on either flank (3). Arquebusiers and gunners firing small versos (swivel guns) gave the *galleasses* extra firepower at short range. With their powerful armament these were formidable opponents and with higher sides than conventional galleys, they were difficult to board. The scene depicts the battle shortly after the first line of the Turkish centre passed the two *galleasses* of the Christian Central Division. In both the northern and central sectors of the battle the Turkish battle line was force to divide into three to pass the *galleasses*. The natural tendency to shy away from these powerful ships led the Turkish galleys to bunch up, disrupting their battle line and slowing their advance. Here the right wing of the Turkish Centre (4) has passed the northernmost *galleass* of the pair attached to the Christian Centre. The Turkish galleys that passed closest to these Venetian giants suffered considerable damage in the process. The disordered Turkish first line then engaged the Christian centre (5). The *galleasses* waited to engage the Turkish reserves (6) that followed on behind the first line, inflicting further damage on the Ottoman galleys. They then turned around and attacked the rear of the Turkish fleet, which by this stage was locked in its brutal fight with the main Christian battle line. (Tony Bryan)

'The Battle of Lepanto', a fresco by Giorgio Vasari. Christian arquebusiers and Turkish archers face each other in the centre of the composition, while two distinct melees are fought in the distance, representing the fighting in the central and northern sectors. Palazzo del Vatican, Rome. (Stratford Archive)

the Turkish galleys as it sought to reinforce the flagship. By pushing the *Faith* and *Hope* of Venice between the Turkish reserves and the flagship, Don Álvaro succeeded in preventing the flow of Turkish reinforcements onto Ali Pasha's flagship. An unnamed Spanish galley destroyed a Turkish galley that was manoeuvring to board the *Real*, and the situation in the centre reached a new phase. Unable to reinforce the fleet flagship and use it as a bridge to get at the Christian flagship, the Turks were forced onto the defensive in the central press of ships. Don Álvaro wisely decided to keep the rest of his force in reserve, pending further developments, and moved off towards the right of the Christian central 'Battle', where the *Capitana* of Malta (commanded by Father Giustiano, the Prior of Messina) held the end of the Christian formation.

Don John's men were successfully reinforced, and repulsed the Turks from the Christian flagship. By 12.20pm the fight had surged onto Ali Pasha's flagship, and for the next 30 or 40 minutes the Christians launched three successive assaults against the Turkish flagship. After the first was repulsed, Amurat Dragut Rais, commanding the Turkish reserve division, managed to fight his way through the press of ships and reinforced Ali Pasha's flagship. Two more Christian assaults were also repulsed, as were two more on Pertau Pasha's *Capitana*. Observers recall the horrendous scene, with the water filled with men, flotsam, entrails and blood. This see-saw battle continued until about 12.30pm, when Marco Antonio Colonna finally managed to overcome Turkish resistance on Pertau Pasha's galley. Pertau Pasha had been badly burned by an incendiary device, and when a *fusta* took him off his flagship to safety, morale on his galley seemed to crumble. Colonna's Flag Captain, Remegasso, prompted his commander for fresh orders, exclaiming: 'This galley is ours. Shall we look for another, or aid the *Real*?' Colonna elected to go to the aid of his fleet commander. The Papal *Capitana* steered through the melee, and smashed into the bow of the Turkish

The climax of the battle. Christian superiority in both ordnance and small-arms fire proved decisive, and this superiority is reflected in the carving. The galley in the left foreground carries three large pieces in her bow battery. Bas relief from the Basilica Santa Maria Maggiore, Rome. (Stratford Archive)

Sultana with such force that the two bows locked. A devastating volley of bow guns and small-arms fire was followed by a surge of troops over the bows of the Turkish galley. The tide had turned, and Don John's men once again attempted to board the Turkish flagship further aft. Caught between the two groups of Christian soldiers, the remaining Turkish defenders were overwhelmed, and cut down. Don John's men cut down the Turkish standards, prompting cheering throughout the Christian centre.

It is unclear what happened to Ali Pasha in those final moments, around 1.00pm. It seems most likely that he was badly wounded in the final stage of the fighting and killed by a Spanish soldier. Accounts have the soldier cutting off Ali Pasha's head, then offering it to Don John as a prize. Don John is supposed to have retorted, 'What am I to do with it?' but there is nothing to substantiate the story. More likely, he was simply cut down in the melee when no quarter was being given by the Christians, regardless of rank. A more colourful Turkish account has him inflicting a mortal wound on himself, then jumping overboard to avoid capture, but this seems out of keeping with the admiral, who would have been more likely to fight on to the last.

This was the real turning point of the battle. As Don John's *Real* took the Turkish *Sultana* in tow as a prize the fighting ebbed in the centre, as the Turks realised that their commander had been killed. They were also running out of ammunition. One report mentions them throwing fruit at the Christians, as they had no more arrows or shot. Some managed to back water and escape, but most of the Turkish galleys were too intermingled with their opponents to flee. Along the whole mile-long line of the central portion of the battle, Turkish *fustas* carried

off survivors, and those left on board either surrendered or were cut

Angels of victory bear laurel leaves of victory in this Papal fresco commemorating the battle. In the left centre, Don John is pictured surrounded by Spanish and Imperial standards, surveying the destruction of the Turkish fleet from the bow of his flagship. Palazzo del Vatican, Rome. (Stratford Archive)

down by a resurgent Christian tide. All the Turkish ships in the very centre of the battle were captured or sunk by 1.20pm, while fighting on the two wings of the central battle continued for another ten minutes, before the Turks began surrendering *en masse*. While prisoners were taken, the majority of the Turkish crews were massacred, or were forced to fight on to the last. The scene must have been indescribable, as the blood lust of the Christian soldiers after nearly 90 minutes of hand-to-hand fighting meant that few prisoners were likely to be taken. The waters swarmed with men, and Christian pikemen stabbed at the survivors in the sea, ignoring cries for help. Others pillaged whatever they could from their Turkish prizes, passing from galley to galley, until many of the Christian ships in the centre were virtually unmanned. Officers tried to rally their men, but it proved an impossible task. Victory for the Christians in the north and centre had been assured and nothing more could be asked of the men. Meanwhile, the battle continued further to the south.

In another detail of the painting featured earlier, a small Spanish galley brings reinforcements up from the reserve squadron to the line of Christian ships in the centre of the picture. The reinforcement of the centre by Don Álvaro de Bazán played a vital part in the Christian victory. Detail from 'The Battle of Lepanto', a painting by the Italian School, late 16th century. (National Maritime Museum, Greenwich, London)

ANDREA DORIA vs ULUCH ALI

In the opening moves of the battle, Uluch Ali swung his ships to port, steering south-west. Andrea Doria promptly responded by wheeling his 'Battle' to starboard, in an attempt to counter any threat to his open right flank. These manoeuvres meant that the Christian right wing and Turkish left wing were separated from the central divisions to the north, and also lagged behind the rest of the fleet. This meant that the clash in the south would take place after those in the north and centre. Turning over 50 ships took time, which Doria hoped would allow the two *galleasses* attached to his wing to reach their allotted positions. Although three or four galleys of the vanguard towed each, none reached further than the southern edge of the central 'Battle' before Uluch Ali and Andrea Doria finally clashed, shortly after noon.

Andrea Doria was aware that Uluch Ali's force outnumbered him by over 40 vessels, although many were small, light, Barbary *galiots* rather than full-sized galleys. Ideal for raiding and skirmishing, they were ill suited for service in a major naval battle. This said, their big advantage was speed, and Uluch Ali planned to use this to outmanoeuvre his opponent, sweeping around his flank and enveloping it. The commanders were well matched, as Andrea Doria and Uluch Ali were both experienced seamen and skilled commanders, and both realised the importance of the open flank. As a light westerly breeze was springing up, the Turks would be placed at a slight disadvantage, having to row into the wind. The effects of this would be minimised if the Turkish galleys looped south, then approached their opponents from the south or south-east. Uluch Ali was well aware that Andrea Doria's reaction to his manoeuvres would open a gap in the Christian line. He most probably assumed that due to his preponderance of faster, lighter vessels, he would be better placed to use this to his

RIGHT **A launch filled with Turkish survivors overturns through overcrowding at the end of the battle. Turkish crewmen who were able to swim were soon summarily drowned or executed by the victorious Christians. Detail from a contemporary German engraving dated 1575. (Author's Collection)**

advantage. The widening gap in the Christian line certainly alarmed Don John, who sent a *galley* to Andrea Doria, requesting him to re-form on the right flank of the Christian centre. By the time the messenger arrived, the situation had changed.

By noon the two wings were about a mile apart, but Uluch Ali had already decided he would be unable to outflank his wily opponent. He ordered his galleys to turn to starboard, heading for the wide gap in the Christian line. Uluch was steering his force to the north-west, while Andrea Doria was continuing on a eastward course, presumably in his own attempt to outflank the Turkish left wing. The movements of both wings were slow, prompting suggestions of treachery aimed at both Andrea Doria and Uluch Ali by their colleagues to the north. Shortly after noon, a group of 12 Venetian galleys, two Spanish (Sicilian), one Savoyard and one Papal galley broke away from the rest of the fleet, apparently without permission from Andrea Doria. The senior Christian officer in the group was Giovanni di Cardona, commanding the *Capitana* of Sicily. They turned to the left, then increased speed in an attempt to intercept the right wing of Uluch Ali's force. This left Andrea Doria with just 35 galleys. Uluch Ali saw the move and realised it presented him with a great opportunity to isolate a portion of the Christian fleet. He ordered his division to wheel round even further to starboard, increasing speed to intercept the break-away Christian galleys. This means that somewhere in the region of 75 Turkish galleys made contact with a mere 16 Christian vessels, at or soon after 12.20pm. Andrea Doria was powerless to intervene, as the Turks were closer to the isolated galleys than he was. The Christians did manage to gain the support of one of the two *galleasses* attached to Andrea Doria's wing. As the *galleass* of Andrea da Cesaro was a few hundred yards south-west of the Christian centre, it was well placed to fire in support of the isolated galleys, some 300 yards (275m) to the south-east. The second *galleass* was about 800 yards (730m) astern of

The Turkish crew flee from a galley that is being overpowered by the Christians in the central engagement. The final stages of the battle saw a wholesale slaughter of Turkish survivors, as the Turkish reserve squadron was unable to rescue more than a fraction of the combatants. Detail from a contemporary German engraving, dated 1575. (Author's Collection)

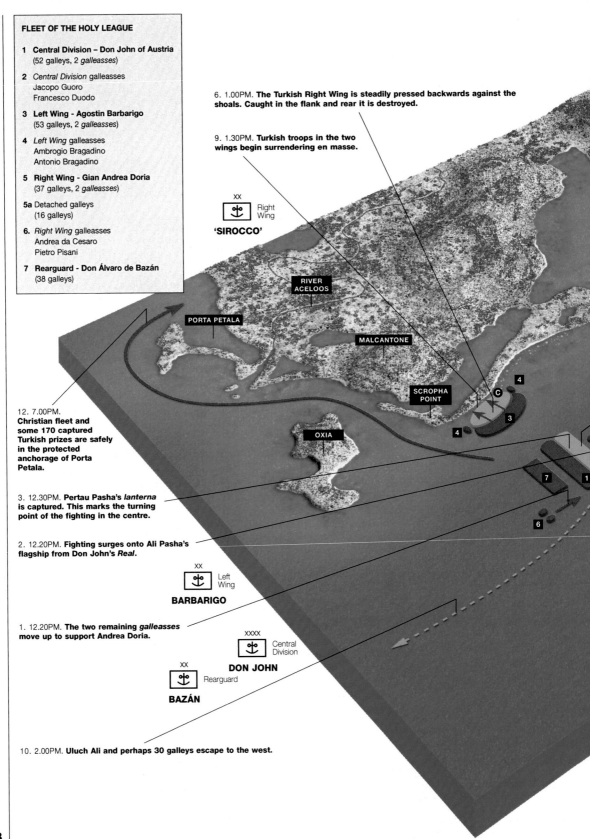

FLEET OF THE HOLY LEAGUE

1 **Central Division – Don John of Austria**
(52 galleys, 2 *galleasses*)

2 *Central Division* galleasses
Jacopo Guoro
Francesco Duodo

3 **Left Wing - Agostin Barbarigo**
(53 galleys, 2 *galleasses*)

4 *Left Wing* galleasses
Ambrogio Bragadino
Antonio Bragadino

5 **Right Wing - Gian Andrea Doria**
(37 galleys, 2 *galleasses*)

5a Detached galleys
(16 galleys)

6. *Right Wing* galleasses
Andrea da Cesaro
Pietro Pisani

7 **Rearguard - Don Álvaro de Bazán**
(38 galleys)

6. 1.00PM. **The Turkish Right Wing is steadily pressed backwards against the shoals. Caught in the flank and rear it is destroyed.**

9. 1.30PM. **Turkish troops in the two wings begin surrendering en masse.**

Right Wing

'SIROCCO'

RIVER ACELOOS

PORTA PETALA

MALCANTONE

SCROPHA POINT

C

4

3

4

OXIA

12. 7.00PM. **Christian fleet and some 170 captured Turkish prizes are safely in the protected anchorage of Porta Petala.**

7

1

3. 12.30PM. **Pertau Pasha's *lanterna* is captured. This marks the turning point of the fighting in the centre.**

6

2. 12.20PM. **Fighting surges onto Ali Pasha's flagship from Don John's *Real*.**

Left Wing

BARBARIGO

1. 12.20PM. **The two remaining *galleasses* move up to support Andrea Doria.**

Central Division

DON JOHN

Rearguard

BAZÁN

10. 2.00PM. **Uluch Ali and perhaps 30 galleys escape to the west.**

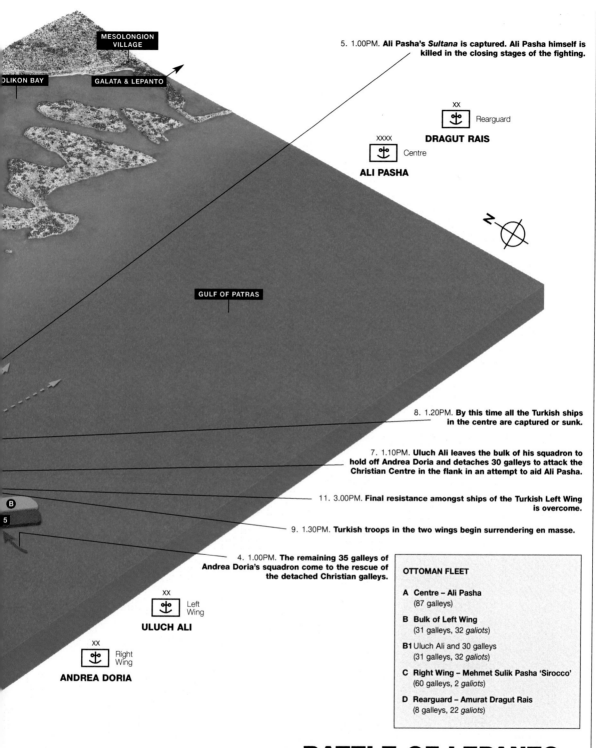

MESOLONGION VILLAGE

OLIKON BAY

GALATA & LEPANTO

5. 1.00PM. **Ali Pasha's *Sultana* is captured. Ali Pasha himself is killed in the closing stages of the fighting.**

XX
⚓ Rearguard
DRAGUT RAIS

XXXX
⚓ Centre
ALI PASHA

GULF OF PATRAS

8. 1.20PM. **By this time all the Turkish ships in the centre are captured or sunk.**

7. 1.10PM. **Uluch Ali leaves the bulk of his squadron to hold off Andrea Doria and detaches 30 galleys to attack the Christian Centre in the flank in an attempt to aid Ali Pasha.**

11. 3.00PM. **Final resistance amongst ships of the Turkish Left Wing is overcome.**

9. 1.30PM. **Turkish troops in the two wings begin surrendering en masse.**

4. 1.00PM. **The remaining 35 galleys of Andrea Doria's squadron come to the rescue of the detached Christian galleys.**

XX
⚓ Left Wing
ULUCH ALI

XX
⚓ Right Wing
ANDREA DORIA

B

5

OTTOMAN FLEET

A Centre – Ali Pasha
   (87 galleys)

B Bulk of Left Wing
   (31 galleys, 32 *galiots*)

B1 Uluch Ali and 30 galleys
   (31 galleys, 32 *galiots*)

C Right Wing – Mehmet Sulik Pasha 'Sirocco'
   (60 galleys, 2 *galiots*)

D Rearguard – Amurat Dragut Rais
   (8 galleys, 22 *galiots*)

BATTLE OF LEPANTO –
DESTRUCTION OF THE TURKISH FLEET

7 October 1571, 12.20pm–7.00pm, viewed from the south-west, showing the annihilation of the Ottoman fleet except for Uluch Ali and some of his galleys who manage to break out and escape. Weather is clear, wind 4–5 knots from west-north-west, tidal movement and currents are negligible.

ABOVE **A popular legend surrounded the battle. Pope Pius V in Rome received a vision on the day of the battle, informing him of the decisive Christian victory. This engraving celebrates the supposed miracle. (Biblioteca Nacionale, Madrid)**

RIGHT **El Greco allegorised the battle of Lepanto in his 'Worship of the Name of Jesus'. While the almighty destroys the 'heathen' Turks with fire and devilish sea monsters, Pope Pius V leads the prayer of the faithful, including Philip II, Don John and the Venetian Doge. (Museo del Prado, Madrid)**

Cesaro, and was unable to help. Cesaro ordered his towing galleys to cut their tow-ropes, and together the force tried to shore up the flank of the Christian centre and to support Cardona and his galleys. Although the supporting fire certainly helped, Cardona and his compatriots were all but overwhelmed. The odds were simply too great, as the Christians were outnumbered five to one. While most of the Christians realised that resistance was foolhardy and surrendered, others refused to give up the fight. One of the Venetian galleys was the *Resurrected Christ* of Venice (IV) commanded by Benedetto Soranzo, who fired the magazine of his own ship when his crew was overwhelmed. The resulting explosion damaged Cardona's *Capitana* of Sicily, but the effect on the Turks was even greater and several galleys were severely damaged by the explosion and fire. Cardona himself was badly burned, and although his crew still held on, it seemed as if the ship would have to surrender. The time was around 1.00pm. At that crucial juncture Andrea Doria arrived with his remaining 35 galleys. He had seen the problem and reacted by turning his force to port, heading roughly east-north-east. He had let Uluch Ali get the better of him, but he also saw the opportunity presented by the Turkish concentration.

The reinforcements ploughed through the scattered remnants of Cardona's galleys, recapturing all but two that had been sunk (these were the *Resurrected Christ* of Venice (IV) and the *Palm* of Candia). Andrea Doria's *Capitana* alone recaptured five of the lost galleys. Uluch Ali pulled his forces back when he saw Andrea Doria approach and, after exchanging fire at long range as the Christians recaptured their galleys, he moved away. He left the bulk of his force to screen Andrea Doria while he led 30 of his galleys northwards to attack the right wing of the Christian centre. He hoped to strike a decisive blow, relieving the pressure on Ali Pasha. He was too late. By this time Ali Pasha was dead and his entire command was disintegrating. The closest Christian galley was the *Capitana* of Malta, a perfect target for the Barbary Corsair, who spent most of his career fighting the Knights of the Order of Malta. In fact, the previous year Uluch Ali captured three Maltese galleys in a single engagement. Uluch Ali came

Philip II lifts his infant son, the Crown Prince Ferdinand, to receive the blessings of victory from the Angel of the Lord in this allegorical celebration of his victory at Lepanto. Ferdinand will be able to enjoy the fruits of victory, while the bound and disrobed Turk in the foreground is vanquished, and consigned to the same level as Philip's pet. Oil painting by Titian. (Museo del Prado, Madrid)

alongside the Maltese flagship supported by two other galleys. The Barbary Corsairs cut their way through the Knights, who were already weakened after fighting and capturing three Turkish vessels of Ali Pasha's central division. This time it was the Muslims who offered little quarter, and only six wounded Maltese survived, including Father Giustiano. Uluch Ali rigged tow lines and returned to his main force, towing the Maltese flagship stern first behind him.

His success was short-lived, as Don Álvaro de Bazán had already committed the remains of his reserves to counter Uluch Ali's southern division. Two Maltese galleys from the centre abandoned the fight to pursue the Corsair, while two of Bazán's Spanish galleys joined in the chase. By this stage Uluch Ali was aware of the fate of the rest of the Turkish fleet, or at least the centre, as it was clear that the few remaining Turkish ships there were being overwhelmed. He still commanded between 25 to 30 galleys, but the rest of his force was now locked into a fight with Andrea Doria's 'Battle'. A swirling melee surrounded Andrea Doria's *Capitana*, pinning his forces. Those galleys of the southern wing with Uluch Ali's were the only element of the Turkish fleet that remained uncommitted, while only a portion of the Christian reserve 'Battle' was also free to manoeuvre. Uluch Ali cut his towing cables, leaving the Maltese *Capitana* to drift. As a final insult to his Christian pursuers he ran the Standard of the Knights of Malta up the mast of his *Capitana*. He then ordered his remaining ships to break through the Christian fleet and escape into the open sea to the west. His moment had passed. If Uluch Ali had managed to come to the rescue of the Turkish centre some 30 minutes earlier, Ali Pasha might have avoided defeat. Now it was too little, too late. Two dozen Turkish galleys could accomplish little or nothing in these circumstances, apart from expend themselves in a last futile gesture. Uluch Ali was too experienced to be seduced by pointless heroics. To him, the survival of a portion of the fleet was more important than any heroic gesture. He elected to run, and not before time. While the Spanish reserve supported by two

Miguel de Cervantes, the writer who penned 'Don Quixote' fought at Lepanto and was wounded in the arm. He was known to his later contemporaries as 'the cripple of Lepanto'. 17th century engraving. (Stratford Archive)

THE FLIGHT OF ULUCH ALI (pages 82–83)

The fighting on the southern flank of the battle had not gone according to plan for either the Christians or Turks. At first Uluch Ali, commanding the Turkish Left Wing, veered south in an attempt to outflank the Christian Right Wing, commanded by Andrea Doria. As it became clear that Andrea Doria had matched his manoeuvre and he would be unable to work round the Christians' southern flank, Uluch Ali saw another opportunity. The manoeuvring had drawn the Christian Right Wing away from the rest of the fleet and the Turkish commander saw the chance to slip part of his force into the gap. Altering course, he led his galleys north-west in what was almost certainly an oblique line. Seeing the apparent danger to the Christian Central Division, a number of captains in Andrea Doria's division decided to take matters into their own hands. They changed course to north-east, breaking away from the main body of the Christian Right Wing in an attempt to intercept Uluch Ali's division. The Turks were now closer to the centre of the battle than Andrea Doria and could engage this isolated force before Andrea Doria could come to its aid. Approximately 75 galleys of Uluch Ali's division clashed with around 16 break-away galleys and surrounded them. What followed was a short but brutal engagement, with each Christian galley outnumbered by roughly four-to-one. The Christians put up a stout fight but were overwhelmed. Andrea Doria raced to attack the rear of Uluch Ali's division and arrived in time to prevent the Turks from escaping with their prizes. The clash degenerated into a melee, but Uluch Ali was already manoeuvring about half of his division out of the fight in order to retain the tactical initiative. His plan may still have been to fall on the flank of the Christian Central Division, but it soon became apparent that the Turkish fleet's flagship had been captured and Turkish resistance in the centre was collapsing. Uluch Ali contented himself with attacking the powerful *Capitana* of the Knights of Malta (1), which anchored the southern end of the main Christian line. The Christian galley was captured after most of the Knights of Malta had been killed. Uluch Ali then took his prize in tow, leading it stern-first away from the fighting in the centre. However, Uluch Ali now realised that the portion of his division still locked in combat with Andrea Doria was outnumbered and faced defeat (2). In addition a group of galleys had broken away from the Christian reserve division and were moving to intercept Uluch Ali's remaining galleys from the north-west. He ordered his men to cut the tow-rope and cast the battered *Capitana* of Malta adrift (3). He then ordered his galleys to raise sail (4) and race for the gap between Andrea Doria's division and the Christian centre. It was a race against time but the wily Turkish commander managed to outdistance his pursuers and escape with his surviving galleys. As a last insult he hoisted the captured standard of the Knights of Malta (5) from the mast of his flagship. (Tony Bryan)

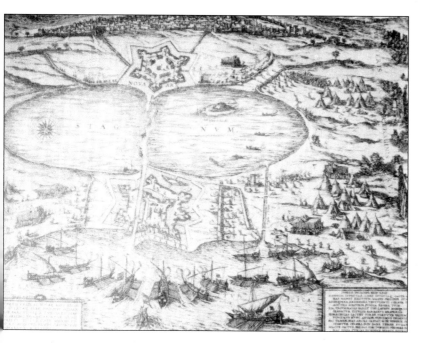

The Barbary port of Tunis was captured by Don John's fleet in 1573, but was recaptured by Uluch Ali's Turkish fleet the following year, thereby denying the Christians any permanent foothold on the Barbary Coast. This engraving depicts the Turkish siege of the Spanish-held port in 1574. (Clyde Hensley Collection)

Don Luis de Requesens (*Comendator Major* of Castille) commanded one of the galleys charged with supporting Don John's flagship in the centre of the Christian main 'Battle'. He prevented the Turks from isolating and defeating the Christian flagship, and was made a Knight of the elite Order of Santiago as a reward for his services. 18th-century painting. (Museo Maritimo, Barcelona)

galleasses was approaching from the north-west, other galleys were approaching his ships from the north.

Accounts tell how Don John and the senior commanders of the Christian central 'Battle' tried to impose order on their fleet, attempting to extricate ships from the mass of vessels in the centre. It was virtually impossible to stop the plundering, and even those galley captains who managed to restrain their crew found themselves torn between duty and reward. In a letter written two days after the battle, the Venetian Sereno recorded that: 'After gaining the day in the centre, His Highness went that way [South], with Colonna. I dropped the galleys I had taken and had to tow to go where help was needed [South]. Some Venetian galleys coming behind boarded my prizes and had much booty, for these Corsairs were very rich. I do not care, for I did not come to rob but to fight and serve Our God.' He added, 'Although the hulls and guns were [later] delivered to us by order of Don John, we got nothing but the honour and fatigue of towing them to Messina.' The same happened to several others.

Uluch Ali realised that the Christians would soon be in a position to prevent the escape of any part of the Turkish fleet, giving them total victory. There is still some controversy surrounding the route taken by Uluch Ali's galleys as they made their escape. Some accounts say he tried to close with the remainder of his galleys, who were busy fighting a losing battle against Andrea Doria. His vessels raised their sails to aid their escape, but as the wind was coming from the west, this meant that the escape route was either north-west or south-west. The commonly held view is the former route was favoured, and that he hoped to beach his galleys off Scropha Point. This said, a westerly course avoided Andrea Doria's ships, the reserves of Bazán and the handful of galleys gathered around Don John. One leading historian favours a circumnavigation of the central 'Battle', sailing behind the position held by Ali Pasha, then making a break due west through a gap between the Christian left wing and centre. What is even more likely was that he headed west-north-west,

The standard of Don John, flown over his *Real* during the battle. This highly ornate and richly embroidered device depicts the crucifixion of Christ on one side and the Virgin Mary on the other. It is one of five standards flown from the flagship during the battle. (Real Armeria de Madrid)

steering as close to the wind as possible. It was a race which several of his rearmost galleys were unable to win. Cut off by Don Álvaro de Bazán's rearguard, they broke off to the north in an attempt to beach themselves. Most were successful, leaving Uluch Ali and perhaps 30 galleys to escape to the west and the rest of the Turkish fleet to be surrounded and forced to surrender or fight to the death. It is unknown when the fighting finally ended, but Uluch Ali probably effected his escape around 2.00pm, and resistance continued amidst the remains of the Turkish southern division for another hour.

Don John expressed a wish to pursue Uluch Ali, but Colonna and his captain, Remegasso, counselled him to remain with the fleet. The wind was rising, the pressure was falling and a storm was expected by nightfall. It was imperative that the badly damaged Christian galleys be sheltered in a safe harbour by nightfall, and that their prizes were also rescued and towed to safety. The battle against the Turks had been won. The battle to save the fleet and its prizes would continue for some time.

Not only were the prizes filled with plunder and prisoners, but the artillery they were fitted with was too valuable to jeopardise. Some of the galleys of both sides were beyond hope, their hulls shattered, their crews dead or wounded and their oars broken. Those vessels not seaworthy were towed to the beach and shoals off Scropha Point and burned during the late afternoon. Don John selected the nearby anchorage of Porta Petala as the fleet's rallying point, and the burning galleys off the Point illuminated the grisly procession of battered hulls as they limped north. The battle was won, but the carnage had been immense. The seas

were gradually cleared of survivors and flotsam, as both sank beneath the waters of the Gulf of Patras, were hauled on board or dispatched by the victors. Over the next three hours the Christian fleet was safely brought into the anchorage, along with some 170 captured Turkish galleys. By 7.00pm the fleet was safely inside the protective headland of Porta Petala, and the sailors and soldiers of the Christian fleet finally took the opportunity to get what rest they could.

The fighting had lasted some four hours, and the survivors were exhausted. Despite this, they were well aware of the importance of their victory and of the decisive nature of the defeat the Turks had suffered. Lepanto was a bloody, hard-fought action, but it was also a decisive one. With the exception of Uluch Ali and a handful of ships, almost the entire Turkish galley fleet had been destroyed in the battle. It must have seemed as if God had answered the prayers of the Christian sailors. Unfortunately for Don John and his commanders, fate would rob the Christians of most of the fruits of their victory.

AFTERMATH

To even the most exhausted survivor of Lepanto, it must have been obvious that the battle had been unusually decisive. The final tally was 170 Turkish galleys captured or sunk, 30,000 Turks killed or wounded, and 3,000 prisoners captured. Other Turkish survivors were scattered across the south-western corner of Greece. Only Uluch Ali and his small force of some 30 galleys escaped the debacle. A further 30 *fustas* and *galiots* managed to escape towards Lepanto as the battle drew to a close, spiriting away another 12,000 Turkish crewmen. In addition over 15,000 Christian galley slaves were freed that day and, by order of Don John and the senior commanders, a celebratory *Te Deum* was sung that evening. Christian losses were light in terms of vessels lost. Only 10 galleys had been sunk, and all captured galleys had been recaptured bar one, which was spirited away by Uluch Ali. By contrast, the human butcher's bill was high. Eight thousand men had been killed during the fighting, and a further 21,000 Christians wounded, meaning that more than one man in three was incapacitated in the fight. Many of the wounded would not survive the week it took to transport them to Corfu. Only the addition of so many former galley slaves to the Christian force enabled it to remain a fleet in being, capable of rowing away from the bloody waters of the Gulf of Patras.

As the Christian leaders gathered on Don John's *Real* to congratulate their commander, the soldiers and sailors exchanged tales of their exploits, or simply thanked God for their own survival. Even Sebastian Venier hugged Don John in an embrace during the commanders' impromptu gathering. The Venetian commander Antonio Duodo was singled out by Don John for special praise. His handling of the six *galleasses* under his command did much to influence the course of the battle. Don John was also charitable towards his enemies, greeting the two sons of Ali Pasha who had been captured during the battle, and commiserated with them on the loss of their father. His attitude towards other Turkish prisoners was less charitable. Many wounded prisoners were slaughtered during the night, including 'Sirocco', who begged to be spared the agony of dying slowly from his wounds. Others were interrogated before being put to the sword, allowing the Christians to build up a better picture of their foes and the size of their defeated force.

His subordinates may have praised him following the victory, but Don John had little opportunity to rest on his laurels. A storm sprang up that evening, and his decimated crews spent an uncomfortable night in Porta Petala, listening to the roaring of the wind and the cries of the wounded. Others storms were also brewing. Rumours had begun to circulate that Andrea Doria had tried to avoid battle, while others accused him of letting Uluch Ali escape. Clearly the Venetian–Genoese

A Turkish banner captured during the battle. It hung vertically from a cross-pole, and its ochre field is decorated by crimson discs and a bar bearing an inscription from the Koran written in gold thread, while further gold stars and edging surround the central device – a stylised representation of the double-pointed 'Sword of Ali'. (Civici Musei Veneziani d'arte e di storia, Venice)

rivalry that had nearly caused the break-up of the League a week before had re-ignited, with new fuel to create dissent in the Christian ranks. With his battered fleet short of supplies of food and water, Don John gave the order for the fleet to sail north on 9 October. The following day his fleet halted to reconnoitre the Turkish-held island of Santa Maura, and to rendezvous with the seventh *galleass*, which had been delayed at Corfu and had missed the battle. The prizes were also divided between the various contingents, according to pre-agreed proportions. With infections from wounds spreading and his men dying by the score, there was no time for delay, and the fleet limped north through a squall which claimed several prizes, finally reaching Corfu on 23 October. With the campaign officially over for the year, the fleet dispersed, the Venetians heading north, and the rest sailing west towards Messina.

The historian Fernand Braudel (1949) called Lepanto 'a victory that led nowhere'. The Holy League failed to capitalise on its triumph. The wily Uluch Ali was appointed as the new Turkish fleet commander, and he supervised the hasty construction of a fleet of 2,000 new Turkish galleys. Although built from green wood, this was a 'fleet in being', and succeeded in denying the Christians the opportunity to consolidate their victory in Greece. The 1572 campaign pitted Don John and his bickering allies against a Turkish commander who knew how to fight defensively, and using the fortresses of Morea (the Peloponnese) to protect him, he held on to Greece, and his fleet. The political division of the alliance thwarted further Christian operations. When Pope Pius died in May 1573, the Holy League lost its staunchest advocate. Although Don John developed plans to sweep through the Aegean Sea as far as the Dardanelles, a combination of Turkish skill and Venetian intransigence made any such venture impractical. He contented himself with the capture of Tunis from the Barbary Corsairs in June 1573, a victory nullified by Uluch Ali's recapture of the port the following year.

This evocative painting focuses on the clash of the two flagships in the foreground while the embroiled fleets fill the rest of the otherwise fictitious seascape. While the setting is inaccurate, the galleys are clearly drawn by an artist who has witnessed them in action. 'The Battle of Lepanto', a painting by the Italian School, late 16th century. (National Maritime Museum, Greenwich, London)

When the Venetians signed a peace treaty with the Ottoman Turks in April 1573, all further hopes of concerted action by the Holy League were dashed. The Venetians were the primary benefactors of the Holy League, as the alliance helped prevent the collapse of the entire Venetian overseas empire. With their territories safeguarded, the next Venetian priority was the resumption of trade, not the continuation of a costly 'crusade'. Cyprus remained in Turkish hands, although the one significant outcome of the 1572 campaign was the safeguarding of Crete, which was heavily reinforced by Venetian troops.

Guilmartin (2001) goes further. He emphasises that in the Mediterranean, naval doctrines used everywhere else were never applicable. The Atlantic notions of maritime control and naval supremacy failed to stand up to the shifting politics and delicate economic balance of the Renaissance Mediterranean. To Guilmartin, the greatest achievement of the battle was a moral one. Until Lepanto the Turkish fleet was seen as invincible. Even the defeat at Malta in 1565 failed to make a significant dent in Turkish military and naval prestige – Lepanto shattered this illusion of invincibility. The Turkish losses in ships could be replaced. Harder to replace was the skilled manpower; the veteran galley captains, gunners, *Janissaries* and Barbary Corsairs who perished in the battle. Of the 3,000 prisoners captured, the Venetians executed anyone who showed any level of skill, thereby reducing the Turkish pool of skilled personnel even further. The real architect of the 1570 campaign against Cyprus that precipitated the Lepanto campaign was the Turkish Grand Vizier, Sokullu Mehmed Pasha. After Lepanto he declared: 'The Christians have singed my beard [his fleet], but I have lopped off his arm [Cyprus]. My beard will grow back, but his arm will not.' Although this was true in the short term, as Uluch Ali created a new fleet the following year, it was no longer the veteran force that confronted the Christians at Lepanto. After his brilliant coup in recapturing Tunis in 1574, Uluch Ali and his raw fleet were kept on the strategic defensive. With her offensive arm blunted, the Ottoman Turks lost the initiative in the Mediterranean and would never recover it. From that point on, Ottoman history would be a tale of socio-economic decline and military and political stagnation.

THE BATTLEFIELD TODAY

The old adage that 'no flowers grow on a sailor's grave' is as true of Lepanto as any other naval battle. The events of 1571 have long since ceased to have any significance to the fishermen who work in the Gulf of Patras, or to the passengers whose ferries and cruise ships transit the Gulf of Corinth. The sea level in that part of Greece has changed considerably in the intervening four and a half centuries. A survey of water level changes in Greek waters commissioned by UNESCO in 1980 revealed a rise of 1.12m (3.5ft) in the four centuries between 1580 and 1980. Although this has little relevance to the battle itself, its effect on the coastline off which the battle was fought is significant. The coastline around Scropha Point was very low-lying in 1571. Offshore shoals fringed the coast, behind which lay an expanse of salt ponds, leading to the volcanic outcrop of Malcantone. This low-lying area is unchanged, save that the rising water level has pushed the coastline back by almost 800 metres (875yds). Further to the east, the labyrinth of coastal sand flats, salt pans, salt ponds and estuarine water has extended the Mesolongi Inlet two miles (3.2km) inland, and much of the area leading to it has been submerged, creating an area of shallow water now referred to as the Mesolongi Lagoon. The sea level change is particularly noticeable around Porta Petala. The anchorage where the Christian fleet spent the night of 7 October has since been inundated, and Petala Point has now become an island, not the mouth of a natural harbour. Apart from that, this quiet corner of Greece has remained largely unchanged. Beneath the slopes of Mount Arakinthos the coastal town of Mesolongi has changed little, apart from its inclusion as a halt on a railway linking the industrial town of Agrinio further to the north with the modern lading facility of Krioneri to the south-east. The castle of Lepanto (now Naupactos), where the Turkish commanders held their council of war three days before the battle, still exists. Similar fortifications that played a part in the campaign are still in existence in Famagusta, Corfu and Santa Maura.

An underwater archaeological survey of the battlefield was conducted in the 1970s, and it revealed a host of potential targets during a magnetometer sweep of the waters off Scropha Point. This revealed the presence of ironwork, prompting a further sonar survey, which showed the presence of non-ferrous clumps, which most probably mark the location of the bow armament of sunken galleys. We know that at least 30 galleys were lost in this relatively small area, and this is reflected in the density and the distribution of targets. The waters of the Gulf of Patras are relatively shallow, and as most wrecks lie in a depth of less than 150 metres (450ft), archaeological investigation is eminently possible. The Greek Government passed draconian laws, making non-government sponsored underwater investigation illegal. As most underwater projects in the Aegean and Ionian

seas have concentrated on Classical shipwrecks and submerged sites, the Lepanto wrecks still lie on the seabed, waiting for a future generation to reveal their secrets.

Turning to the ships themselves, the Mediterranean basin is well served by maritime museums and national collections which reveal something of the splendour of Renaissance galleys of the Lepanto period. The Museo Maritimo (now the Museu Maritim) in Barcelona is a particularly fine example, housed in the Drassanes Reales (Royal Shipyard), a series of buildings which once served as galley sheds, built in the 13th century. The centrepiece of the museum is a full-scale replica of Don John of Austria's *Real* as it would have appeared on that fateful day in October 1571. Other artefacts tell the story of the Spanish contribution to the Holy League, and describe the campaign. A similar story is presented in the Museo Naval in

In this detail of the allegorical painting of the battle by Giorgio Vasari, the Venetian *galleasses* are shown between the two main battle lines, facing the oncoming wave of Turkish galleys. (Civici Musei Veneziani d'arte e di storia, Venice)

Madrid. A magnificent variety of ship models, paintings and plans are housed in this superb collection, but visitors will be especially fascinated by the artefacts which relate directly to the battle, such as the stern lantern from Don Álvaro de Bazán's *Capitana*, the flagship of the Christian reserve squadron.

In Venice, the Musco Storico Navale houses a similar collection, including spectacular models of Venetian galleys of the late 16th century and detailed depictions of the *galleasses* that fought in the battle. It also traces the story of the Venice Arsenal and its long tradition of galley building. Another worthwhile collection in the city is the Civici Musei Veneziani d'art e di storia (The Civic Art and History Museum), which contains numerous paintings depicting the battle. Similar artistic depictions can be found in the National Maritime Museum, London and in the Museo del Prado in Madrid. Finally the Topkapi Museum in Istanbul contains a valuable collection of Turkish ship models dating from the late 17th century. The author was unable to visit the Musee Navale di Genova Pegli before completing this work, but the museum houses a widely acclaimed collection of maritime artefacts from the period, and a display covering the Doria dynasty of naval *condottieri*.

BIBLIOGRAPHY

While several non-English works have been consulted while researching the material presented in this book, only the secondary works that are widely available in English have been listed here. Guilmartin (1974) and Gardiner (ed.) (1995) both contain extensive bibliographies listing these non-English sources, as well as more extensive lists of works on more specialised aspects of the Lepanto story, such as galley construction and ordnance.

Anderson, R.C.; *Naval Wars in the Levant, 1559–1853* (Liverpool, 1952)

Anderson, R.C.; *Oared Fighting Ships from Classical Times to the coming of Steam* (Kings Langley, 1976)

Braudel, Fernand; *The Mediterranean and the Mediterranean World in the Age of Philip II* (2 vols.) (London, 1975). First published in France, 1947

Brummet, P.; *Ottoman seapower and Levantine diplomacy in the Age of Discovery* (Albany, NY, 1994)

Elliott, J.H.; *Imperial Spain, 1469–1716* (London, 1970). First published in 1963

Gardiner, Robert (ed.); *The Age of the Galley: Mediteranean Oared Vessels since pre-Classical times.* (London, 1995)

Glete, Jan; *Navies and Nations: Warships, navies and state building in Europe and America, 1500–1860* (Stockholm, 1993)

Glete, Jan; *Warfare at Sea, 1500–1650: Maritime Conflicts and the Transformation of Europe* [Routledge Warfare and History Series] (London, 2000)

Guilmartin, John F., Jr.; *Gunpowder and Galleys: Changing Technology and Mediterranean Warfare at Sea in the Sixteenth Century* (Cambridge, 1974)

Guilmartin, John F., Jr.; 'The tactics of the Battle of Lepanto clarified: The impact of social, economic and political factors on sixteenth century galley warfare' in Craig L. Symonds (ed.) *New Aspects of Naval History* (Annapolis, 1981)

Guilmartin, John F., Jr.; *Galleons and Galleys* [Cassell's History of Warfare Series] (London, 2001)

Hale, J.R. (ed.); *Renaissance Venice* (Totowa, N.J.), 1973)

Hale, J.R.; 'Men and Weapons: The Fighting Potential of Sixteenth Century Renaissance Galleys' in B. Bond & I. Roy (ed.); *War and Society: A Yearbook of Military History* (London 1975)

Hess, A.C; 'The Battle of Lepanto and its place in Mediterranean History' in *Past and Present* Vol. 53 (1973)

Konstam, Angus; 'Sixteenth century naval gunnery and tactics' in *International Journal of Nautical Archaeology* Vol. 17 (1988)

Konstam, Angus (et al.); *Warships: From the Galley to the Present Day* (London, 2001)

Konstam, Angus; *Renaissance War Galleys* (Oxford, 2002)

Lane, Frederic C.; 'Venetian Naval Architecture about 1550' in *Mariners' Mirror* Vol. XX (1934)

Mallett, M.B., & Hale, J.R.; *The Military Organisation of the Renaissance State: Venice, c.1400 to 1617* (Cambridge, 1984)

Marx. Robert F; *The Battle of Lepanto, 1571* (New York, 1966)

Oman, Sir Charles; *A History of the Art of War in the Sixteenth Century* (London 1991). First published in Britain in 1937.

Pryor, John H.; *Geography, Technology and War: Studies of the Maritime History of the Mediterranean, 649–1571* (Cambridge, 1988)

Rabb, Theodore K.; 'Artists at War: Titian's Allegory of the Battle of Lepanto' in *Military History Quarterly* Vol. 11 (1999)

Rodgers, William L.; *Naval Warfare under oars: A study of Strategy, Tactics and Ship Design* (Annapolis, MD, 1980). First published in 1947

Thurbon, Colin (et al.); *The Venetians* [Time Life Mariners' Series] (Amsterdam, 1980)

INDEX